U.S. Foreign Policy and the Crisis of Humanity

By Daniel Silver

Other books by Daniel Silver:

Art & Policies for a Better World

Unravelling the Puzzle of the Los Angeles Times –
Filling in the Missing Pieces to the Stories They Tell

Table of Contents:

Introduction

In 2002 my wife got a dish television receiver. She was changing channels when we came upon a show that we had never heard of before called Democracy Now. Scott Ritter was being interviewed. He was a high level official, one of the people in charge of the United Nations weapons inspection program in Iraq, and he had been there for about seven years. Scott Ritter noted that there is no way that Iraq could have any appreciable amount of weapons of mass destruction. This was before the war had broken out. Then he said another thing that really surprised me – that no main-stream station will give him an interview.

This really demonstrated to me that perhaps things are not quite as they seem. I continued to watch Democracy Now and I read all of the books of many of their guests, and found many other books that were referenced in those books. I became an avid reader and I have been so now for about the last 15 years.

Essentially what I discovered in all this reading is that the vast majority of the general public is being robbed by the wealthiest members of our society, and that the working poor, along with 99% of the entire general public living in the United States can consider themselves lucky, as compared with the masses of people living in third world countries, who are also being robbed, but to a much greater degree.

This book looks at the foreign policy establishment as embodied by the Council on Foreign Relations, and as expressed in their magazine Foreign Affairs.

Works from Foreign Affairs Magazine are referenced, disassembled and then disputed using verifiable and well documented facts.

This work explains much of what the United States is aiming for in its foreign policy.

I reveal many of the methodologies used by the U.S. government, along with many of the motivations for their actions.

I identify where the pool of people who are responsible are derived from.

I make clear who are the victims.

My book very carefully explains in a well-documented manner which eliminates any controversy, how U.S. foreign policy is undoubtedly, a crime spree directed against the world's poor.

I expound on many different ways to correct the behavior of the United States government.

Currently, only five or six corporations own about 90% of the mass media in the United States. Their business plan is to sell advertising to other major corporations on their networks.

According to one estimate, corporations now control about 50% of the entire wealth of the planet. Main stream news is not going to provide its audience with the type of facts and analysis that are found for example, in this volume.

In fact, Jane Akre and her husband Steve Wilson, former reporters on a television station were fired after refusing to knowingly include false information in one of their reports. The false information had to do with ignoring a potential public health hazard caused by a product of a major corporation.

The fired employees successfully sued under Florida's whistle blower law, however, after an appeal was filed by the television station, the whistle blower case was over turned in favor of the television station. The court declared that the Federal Communications Commission policy against news falsification is only a policy and is not a law, therefore, the whistle blower status did not apply. Therefore, there is no law against falsification of news to the general public.

So basically, with this example, I am trying to explain how a book such as this one could come about in the first place.

The following is a brief synopsis of what is covered in the following chapters:

Chapter 1:   U.S. Foreign Policy and the Crisis of Humanity

The history of the establishment of the Council on Foreign Relations is discussed. The big money interests behind it, which guides its policy prescriptions are noted.

I discuss opinion polls which show that the concerns and priorities of the general public and the concerns and priorities of our foreign policy establishment comprise two completely different sets of standards.

Chapter II: Why Latin America is Primed to Explode

I look at an article from Foreign Affairs magazine titled: "Why Latin America was Primed to Explode". Their article discusses a recent wave of massive protests in

Latin America. It looks at the possibility of foreign meddling and calls out Cuba and Venezuela as foreign meddlers, and concludes that foreign meddling could not have been enough to cause that much unrest, and that economic malaise is deemed to be the culprit.

I disagree with their analysis, explaining that foreign meddling is indeed the cause of the unrest, but that the foreign meddler is none other than the United States. I discuss in detail how the World Trade Organization, the International Monetary Fund and the World Bank operate, and how those policies are the proximate cause of a growth in world poverty.

Chapter 3   Let Russia be Russia

I reviewed an article from Foreign Affairs magazine titled: "Let Russia be Russia".

I showed in a number of examples of how the article contradicted itself on several points. I pointed out a number of suggestions that were made by this author that I agreed with and I hypothesized that the article had to be written in this way because of the anti-Russian atmosphere throughout main stream reporting, and that this is a main stream publication, so the author has to go along with the current in order to in the end, make constructive suggestions.

I was able to quote three very well known economists who explained how the West set up Russia for a great fall upon their change from Communism to Capitalism, as Russia had appealed to the U.S. and other Western powers for help in their transition from communism to capitalism.

I was able to refute the charge that Russia had interfered in U.S. elections with evidence from a former Technical Director for the World Geopolitical and Military Analysis for the NSA, a former Senior Analyst of the NSA's Signt Automation Research Center, a former Technical Director in the NSA's office of Signal Processing, along with former Chief of CIA's Soviet Foreign Policy Branch. These people examined the DNC computer which had reportedly been hacked, and concluded that this was an inside job, that the contents of this DNC computer were copied, not through an internet hack, but by a physical device plugged into the computer.

Quotes were provided from the Vice-President of advertising for Facebook which refuted the charge that Facebook was being used by the Russian government to try to influence the American presidential election of 2016.

Chapter 4:   The Age of Great Power Competition

The author of this article in Foreign Affairs Magazine expresses the idea of wanting the U.S. to be the sole superpower. The author states: "The United States central objective should be to keep large states in both regions from gaining so much influence as to shift the local balance of power in their favor." I argue that for many reasons, this is a game that is both dangerous and immoral. The author expresses that the U.S. should use sanctions to punish Russian aggressive actions in Syria, and I explain that it was the Syrian government who had invited Russia to help them to fight Isis. Therefore, why sanctions? And much more is covered in this chapter.

Chapter 5   On the New Intervention Delusion

A Foreign Affairs article "On the New Intervention Delusion" by Richard Fontaine is reviewed. Richard Fontaine is the CEO of the Center for a New American Security, and he has worked for the State Department, the National Security Council, and he was a foreign policy advisor for Senator John McCain.

I pointed out that this author had very seriously misrepresented four major historical events:

The war in Syria

The war in Afghanistan

The war in Libya

The war in Yugoslavia

My rebuttle of the article was accompanied with fully documented evidence and facts which very clearly contradicted the author in several different ways which re-define the very nature of those conflicts.

Chapter 6   The Two Venezuelas

A series of articles about Venezuela is presented by Foreign Affairs, which denigrates the independently verified spectacular successes of Venezuela under the Chavez and then Maduro governments.

I pointed out that a number of years ago, the U.S. invaded an oil rich nation, Iraq, under false pretenses and was able thus to gain control of much of their oil wealth. Denigrating the leadership is the first step towards making the public more amenable to a U.S. intervention.

These articles laid bare the truly evil character of the Council on Foreign Relations and U.S. foreign policy in general. The articles were peppered with lies which I responded to in numerous occasions, using well documented facts.

The articles are called out for their lies and international agencies are cited which reveal the extent of these lies. The lying, it is explained, is because there are people in the U.S. (behind the articles even), who covet the wealth of Venezuela and who want to use the power of the United States government to take that wealth away from those people, throwing them into the abyss, so that those who are already wealthy to begin with, can acquire yet more wealth. And, this chapter is very well documented.

Chapter 7   An Economic Perspective

Chapter 7 discusses economic policies that generate true economic development vs the current policies of the WTO which were drafted by major corporations that had served in an advisory role to the U.S. government in the development of the policies. In earlier chapters I explained how these policies work to the advantage of advanced vs developing countries, and this subject is revisited and further explained in this chapter.

Chapter 8 -Making the World Safe for Democracy

I begin by describing what type of government would be targeted by the U.S. government for destruction. Then I discuss some very huge war crimes committed by the United States government from the past, leading up to today. I follow with a brief discussion on what were the results of European Colonialism on those people who were colonized. I move to a discussion of Geo Politics, citing two important authors, and then discuss some geo-political issues.

Food security is discussed, interwoven with a discussion on the effects of monopoly capitalism in respect to food distribution worldwide, as tied together with the rules of the WTO.

Libya was then discussed and then the chapter moved to a discussion of Africa as a whole. The Middle east was discussed in respect to Pentagon plans which were revealed, and Eastern European activities were briefly examined in respect to U.S. initiatives.

Chapter 9   What We Can Do

Chapter 9 looks at the economic and social inequality in the United States.

Recommendations were proposed in the following areas:

Progressive taxation

Anti-trust enforcement

Break up of giant media corporations

Reversal of Citizens' United

Impeachment of the Supreme Court Justices who ruled for Citizens' United

Campaign Finance Reform – a methodology was detailed

Cessation of the subsidization of the oil industry and instead to subsidize renewable energy companies.

Government funding of alternative media outlets. This is covered more fully in my earlier book.

Enactment of laws requiring media companies to cover elections in much greater detail

Compassion & altruism can be cultivated – added to school curriculum

Changing the corporate charter as described in detail earlier

Have a foreign policy that provides aid to the poor, thus losing enemies and gaining friends, and in the process, saving government funds on over spending for expensive weaponry

Propaganda in our mass media was discussed and the chapter and this book ends with a listing of alternative media sources, followed by suggested readings

Chapter 1.

U.S. FOREIGN POLICY and the Crisis of Humanity – a look at the Council on Foreign Relations and Foreign Affairs Magazine

Modern U.S. foreign policy has been a project fashioned over many decades by the most educated and wealthiest individuals in our society, and in 1921 the Council on Foreign Relations (CFR) was created. In 1922 the Council founded their bi-monthly magazine called Foreign Affairs.

The founders of the Council on Foreign Relations were made up of the captains of industry who wanted to influence U.S. foreign policy in a manner that would maximize the ability of U.S. businesses to expand into foreign markets. The Council, a private corporation, eventually over time became the central policy making establishment of the United States government, and because of the size and power of the United States, the Council became the most influential policy organization in the Western World. The 2007 Council president Richard Haas called the Council "the leading foreign policy organization in the world." Another CFR president Leslie Gelb referred to it as "the world's premier foreign policy organization."

The following accounts seek to demonstrate that, although our foreign policy establishment is staffed with people of high education and high professional achievement, unfortunately this group of people do not share the same level of ethical development as compared with the general public. Although that is not altogether surprising when we take into account that the National Academy of Sciences performed a study which concluded that people in higher socio-economic levels score lower in ethics and ethical behavior.

While our foreign policy establishment has concentrated on grand strategies to increase U.S. power and influence in every corner of the world, Benjamin Page & Marshall Bouton performed a 30-year study that they published in a book titled "The Foreign Policy Disconnect." A major University performed opinion polls over a 30-year period and they concluded that

"Most Americans want a foreign policy that places a high priority on economic and social security at home <u>and Justice abroad.</u>" "Most Americans favor cooperative multi-lateral foreign policies – peaceful, when possible – rather than unilateral military ones." One of their conclusions is that our foreign policy establishment should listen to public opinion more, and to take the views of the public seriously.

Note that similarly, in 2013 the Pew Research Center in association with the Council sent an on-line questionnaire to all CFR members and almost 40% of Council members, 1,838 responded. Then telephone interviews were conducted with 2,003 people representing a cross section of the American public. Many differences were found in what was considered most important. For example, 81% of the general population group felt that protecting American jobs should be considered most important, with only 29% of council members in agreement. On the idea that it was very beneficial when U.S. companies set up operations in foreign countries, 73% of council members agreed, and only 23% of the general public sample agreed. On trade, 93% of Council members were for "free trade" and the

Trans Pacific Partnership, whereas only a small percent of the general public sample was in agreement.

Because these people are highly organized, they are successful at achieving their goals. This book is a call to the general public to learn more about what is being done in our name, and therefore to organize appropriate counter efforts in the name of justice, peace and mutual prosperity among nations. History has shown that when only 1% of the population is politically active, that this is enough to turn the tables in the world of public policy.

I will begin by looking at the Council's history, their personnel and some of their policy prescriptions, and then walk through several of their articles in Foreign Affairs magazine, their mouthpiece. Later chapters will look at other information regarding U.S. foreign policy.

From its creation in 1921 through 1953, the final decision maker in the Council on Foreign Relations, President and Chairman of the Board, always were people who were connected with the Morgan banking group. Then starting in 1953, the final decision maker of the CFR (Council on Foreign Relations), President and Chairman of the Board were Rockefeller connected; first John McCloy from 1953 to 1970 and then David Rockefeller from 1970 to 1985. Peter G Peterson, a billionaire, was the Chairman from 1985 through to 2007.

The Rockefeller family had a history of being highly involved in foreign affairs. On page 29 of Seeds of Destruction by F William Engdahl, he notes that from 1922 to 1926, the Rockefeller foundation donated $410,000.00 to hundreds of German eugenics researchers through their Paris office. In 1926 they awarded $250,000.00 for the creation of the Berlin Kaiser Wilhelm Institute for Psychiatry. That would be the equivalent of 26 million dollars in 2004 dollars and was an unheard of amount considering how Germany was suffering from hyper-inflation. It was eugenics that became the intellectual foundation for the Nazi party and it was the same Rockefeller who was a major founding supporter of the Council on Foreign Relations - who was also the major supporter of eugenics as practiced in Germany in the lead up to the eventual outbreak of World War II.

This organization was and is dominated by the most powerful industrial and financial interests and reflects a classic picture of a conflict of interest, with drivers of Capital striving to make government foreign policy work in concert with their own interests. It can be argued that their definition of the National Interest is actually in reality, a reflection of class interests.

The Council has always employed academic professionals in order to assist them in furthering their views and in their attempt to try to influence public policy decision makers in government , but the academic people have always been a minority group on decision making boards that were and are still made up mostly of corporate board of directors, bankers, and CEO's.

An excellent resource on the CFR and a fantastic book is "Wall Street's Think Tank" by Laurence Shoup. Shoup notes that "The Council is an organization of, by, and for the Plutocracy – and, as indicated by its history, membership, and top leadership, very attuned to the need to incorporate the leading Capitalist Class families." He notes that top leadership of the CFR has very close ties to Wall Street finance capital, and his book goes into great detail to describe a large number of directors of the organization over the years along with many other high ranking members. He concludes that the CFR is: "a top-down Capitalist Class organization representing the system of monopoly finance capitalism."

So this is what drives U.S. foreign Policy!

The Council claims to take no stance in policy and to be utterly objective, but this isn't true. The way they get around this is by convening independent task forces to study subjects of top management's choice, and management picks those individuals who will be on these task forces. These "independent" task forces study key foreign policy issues, reach a consensus, and then publish reports with policy recommendations for policy makers and other readers of Foreign Affairs magazine.

In the year 2000, Foreign Affairs was ranked in a survey as the "most influential of all print media among government decision makers." The 2002 CFR annual report stated "Decision makers in government look to the Council's task forces to help guide their decisions."

In the Reagan administration, 14 out of the 19 foreign policy officials were Council members. In George H.W. Bush's administration 10 of the top 11 foreign policy officials were Council members. In Clinton's administration 15 of the top 17 foreign policy officials were Council members, and under George W Bush 14 of the top 17 foreign policy officials were Council members.

All other major think tank organizations such as the Atlantic Council, the Trilateral Commission, the Brookings Institute, etc., each have several members who are also Council members. Many major corporate board members and media companies have many who are Council members. Many major corporations also hold corporate membership. In 2005 Erdos & Morgan, a business to business research firm performed a survey to document the print media that leaders in government go to for information needed for their work. Foreign Affairs magazine got the number one rating in that category.

To quote once again "Wall Street's Think Tank": "The CFR becomes the formal expression of an exclusive community of, by, and for the capitalist class. It is the central place where this community debates and develops their common worldview, spreading it far and wide through its many members and allied organizations, so that their views become accepted wisdom." Also "The collective function of this effort, led by the Council and the U.S., is to develop a climate of opinion and ideological hegemony about strategic directions for the world plutocracy."

THE COUNCIL'S CONNECTIONS TO THE WAR IN IRAQ

During the Clinton administration through the early years of the first administration of George W., there was a lobby called the Project for the New American Century, which was pushing for war against Iraq. In 1998 this lobby wrote an open letter to President Clinton that argued for the overthrow of Saddam Hussein. Of the 18 people who signed this letter, 12 were Council members. This lobby also argued for an American empire, stating that the role of the U.S. in the world should be comparable to that of England in the 1800's. An analysis of all of the contributors to all of their reports found that of these 68 individuals, 43 of them were members of the Council.

War is good for business, as it provides numerous opportunities. Due to U.S. sanctions, Saddam Hussein was constrained in making any new contracts for oil extraction, but he was planning ahead, talking to several different oil extraction companies, but none of those companies were American.

In Iraq, like Venezuela, much of the oil revenue was directed at providing health care and University schooling to the Iraqi people, but the CEO's of the major oil companies weren't making a dime out of Iraqi students attending college.

After the war there was too much public resistance in Iraq to pass a law to privatize the oil and gas industry, so starting in 2008, the U.S. sponsored Iraqi government simply began to contract with outside oil companies such as Exxon Mobile, Occidental, Royal Dutch Shell, Total SA and more.

Some people have pointed out that in many of these aggressive adventures, that the military costs end up outweighing business benefits, however, it is the U.S. taxpayer who pays for the military costs, and it is the businesses, many of which are able to pay very little taxes, (but pay campaign contributions) who are the beneficiaries.

The key decision makers in the U.S. government who made the decision to go to war with Iraq were mentioned in two books, "America Unbound" by Daalder & Lindsay (both Council members) and "Rise of the Vulcans" by Mann (also a Council member). Twenty one people were named as the people who made the decision for war. Of these 21 people, 18 of them were Council members.

Remember that Council members are made up of corporate heads and directors of multi-national corporations, and also of many major multi-national corporations have corporate membership.

In mid 2002 the Council teamed up with the James A Baker III institute for public policy to establish a 23 member planning group to determine the objectives of such a war along with the post war planning. Then in March of 2003, about nine months later, the war began.

What the U.S. did was to privatize state owned industries and they opened the Iraqi economy, a state-run economy, to a free trade economy virtually overnight. CFR member Paul Bremmer III was appointed by the Bush administration to re-write the rules of the Iraqi economy. His chief economic advisor was a CFR member, M. Peter McPherson. The following is a quote from "Wall Street's Think Tank", an excellent book on the subject;

"Order 12: suspending all trade restrictions, including tariffs and customs duties until 12/31/2003.

Order 37: establishing a 15 percent flat tax

Order 39: re-writing foreign investment laws in favor of foreign multi-national corporations, allowing 100 percent foreign ownership except in the oil sector, privatizing 200 state owned Iraqi enterprises, and allowing unrestricted, tax free repatriation of profits outside of Iraq's borders.

Order 40: Allowing foreign banks to purchase up to 50 percent of an Iraqi bank.

Note that when State industries in a small country are privatized, who has the money needed to buy them? Almost always that will be multi-national corporations, almost certainly located in the United States. So the good news is that a large number of business opportunities were created for U.S. corporations, which is a happy story. The bad part of the story is the mass unemployment which ensued among the Iraqi people which hit between 50 to 60 percent during the summer of 2003.

Perhaps this mass unemployment helps in part to explain more than two million Iraqi deaths.

The book "Giants – The Global Power Elite" by Professor Peter Phillips describes the situation of how the major corporations invest in each other, and how Capital has become so concentrated and over accumulated that investment opportunities become ever harder to find to the point where only three methods appear for the investment of what Phillips calls "excess Capital": risky financial speculation, wars and post wars along with their preparation, and the privatization of state run institutions and enterprises.

Also, by the way, the book "Giants" has this to say about the CFR:

"(The Council of Foreign Relations) (is the premier policy group for international affairs in the United States)." "CFR has a long history of promoting U.S. expansionism, with the goal of solidifying the United States' global hegemonic power." "CFR has historically viewed international affairs from the perspective of U.S. interests." "CFR is strongly neoliberal and free trade oriented."

And U.S. Foreign Policy is and has been very violent and aggressive. Historian William Blum points out the following in his Anti-Empire Report and in his books, and this is a re print from his Anti-Empire Report:

"Since the end of World War 2, the United States has:

- Attempted to overthrow more than 50 foreign governments, most of which were democratically-elected.
- Dropped bombs on the people of more than 30 countries.
- Attempted to assassinate more than 50 foreign leaders.

- Attempted to suppress a populist or nationalist movement in 20 countries.
- Grossly interfered in democratic elections in at least 30 countries.
- Though not as easy to quantify, has also led the world in torture; not only the torture performed directly by Americans upon foreigners, but providing torture equipment, torture manuals, lists of people to be tortured, and in-person guidance by American instructors.

Instances of the United States overthrowing, or attempting to overthrow, a foreign government since the Second World War. (* indicates successful ouster of a government)

- China 1949 to early 1960s
- Albania 1949-53
- East Germany 1950s
- Iran 1953 *
- Guatemala 1954 *
- Costa Rica mid-1950s
- Syria 1956-7
- Egypt 1957
- Indonesia 1957-8
- British Guiana 1953-64 *
- Iraq 1963 *
- North Vietnam 1945-73
- Cambodia 1955-70 *
- Laos 1958 *, 1959 *, 1960 *
- Ecuador 1960-63 *
- Congo 1960 *
  - France 1965

- Brazil 1962-64 *
- Dominican Republic 1963 *
- Cuba 1959 to present
- Bolivia 1964 *
- Indonesia 1965 *
- Ghana 1966 *
- Chile 1964-73 *
- Greece 1967 *
- Costa Rica 1970-71
- Bolivia 1971 *
- Australia 1973-75 *
- Angola 1975, 1980s
- Zaire 1975
- Portugal 1974-76 *
- Jamaica 1976-80 *
- Seychelles 1979-81
- Chad 1981-82 *
- Grenada 1983 *
- South Yemen 1982-84
- Suriname 1982-84
- Fiji 1987 *
- Libya 1980s
- Nicaragua 198
- Panama 1989 *
- Bulgaria 1990 *
- Albania 1991 *
- Iraq 1991
- Afghanistan 1980s *
- Somalia 1993
- Yugoslavia 1999-2000 *

- Ecuador 2000 *
- Afghanistan 2001 *
- Venezuela 2002 *
- Iraq 2003 *
- Haiti 2004 *
- Somalia 2007 to present
- Honduras 2009 *
- Libya 2011 *
- Syria 2012
- Ukraine 2014 *

Instances since the Second World War of the United States attempting to suppress a populist or nationalist movement.

- China – 1945-49
- France – 1947 *
- Italy – 1947-1970s *
- Greece – 1947-49 *
- Philippines – 1945-53 *
- Korea – 1945-53 *
- Haiti – 1959 *
- Laos – 1957-73
- Vietnam – 1961-73
- Thailand – 1965-73 *
- Peru – 1965 *
- Dominican Republic – 1965 *
- Uruguay – 1969-72 *
- South Africa – 1960s-1980s
- East Timor – 1975-1999 *

- Philippines – 1970s-1990s *
- El Salvador – 1980-92 *
- Colombia – 1990s to early 2000s *
- Peru – 1997 *
- Iraq – 2003 to present ** successful suppression

United States bombing of other countries;

The bombing list:

- Korea and China 1950-53 (Korean War)
- Guatemala 1954
- Indonesia 1958
- Cuba 1959-1961
- Guatemala 1960
- Congo 1964
- Laos 1964-73
- Vietnam 1961-73
- Cambodia 1969-70
- Guatemala 1967-69
- Grenada 1983
- Lebanon 1983, 1984 (both Lebanese and Syrian targets)
- Libya 1986
- El Salvador 1980s
- Nicaragua 1980s
- Iran 1987
- Panama 1989
- Iraq 1991 (Persian Gulf War)
- Kuwait 1991

- Somalia 1993
- Bosnia 1994, 1995
- Sudan 1998
- Afghanistan 1998
- Yugoslavia 1999
- Yemen 2002
- Iraq 1991-2003 (US/UK on regular basis)
- Iraq 2003-2015
- Afghanistan 2001-2015
- Pakistan 2007-2015
- Somalia 2007-8, 2011
- Yemen 2009, 2011
- Libya 2011, 2015
- Syria 2014-2016

Note that William Blum passed away in 2018, and this list was compiled in 2016. He authored 4 books, and "Killing Hope" was a 470 page encyclopedic approach to reporting on U.S. foreign interventions.

The United states also interferes in elections in foreign countries. Below is a headline and the first sentence from a 12/21/16 article in the Los Angeles Times:

The U.S. is no stranger to interfering in the

elections of other Countries

By NINA AGRAWAL l.a. times

; The U.S. has a long history of attempting to influence presidential elections in other countries – it's done so as many as 81 times between 1946 and 2000, according to a database amassed by political scientist Dov Levin of Carnegie Mellon University.

So what has been the result of these aggressive actions by the United States over the years? On page 56 of "Dismantling the Empire" by Professor Chalmers Johnson, he writes:

"The Federation of American Scientists has compiled a list of more than two hundred overseas military operations from the end of World War II until September 11, 2001, in which we were involved and typically struck the first blow. The current wars in Afghanistan and Iraq are not included. **In no instance did democratic governments come about as a direct result of any of these military activities.**"

On Global Warming, I would like once more to quote from "Wall Street's Think Tank" which is highly recommended reading to those whose interests include justice and peace;

"The Council, speaking through its study groups, has argued that human-caused global warming is happening, and that something should be done. But *that something* has only been the promotion of a weak cap-and-trade program. This was as far as the CFR was willing to go as of 2014, while continuing to strongly support fracking and the exploitation of the dirty oil of the Canadian tar sands."

Thus, it is not controversial to say, if science matters, that the Council on Foreign Relations, is most certainly the enemy of all of mankind. Therefore, the United States, because of its current foreign policy, is the enemy not only of all of mankind, but also of all complex life on planet earth. Later in this volume, we will discuss the reasons why there are no compelling reasons why our foreign policy must be formulated in this manner.

Earlier it was mentioned that many of those same elite individuals who are members of the CFR are also members of many powerful think tanks and media corporations.

The American Enterprise Institute has been called the premier **conservative** think tank. Three of its 27 trustees are CFR members, including former head of Exxon Mobile Lee Raymond, and former Vice President Dick Cheney. Newt Gingrich is also a council member.

Note that people in the Foreign Policy establishment, the military, and high level corporate executives, tend strongly to be politically conservative.

It is important to more fully understand **Conservatism**.

"People on the right have higher authoritarianism scores than do people on the left." Pratto

Felicia Pratto of the University of Connecticut, co-author of "Social Dominance: An Intergroup Theory of Social Hierarchy and Oppression" wrote the following:

"Just as authoritarianism theorists speculated, there really does appear to be a phenomenon we may call generalized ethnocentrism, reflecting itself in the denigration of a wide range of outgroups, including ethnic groups, political groups, sexual orientation groups, and stigmatized religious groups. Second, this generalized tendency to stigmatize and denigrate the generalized "other" contains a consistent theme of dominance and submission. Third, generalized ethnocentrism is positively associated with political conservatism. This association has been found consistently across a wide variety of cultures and has been found so consistent that some theorists have even considered ethnocentrism as a definitional component of conservatism."

Let's look at an article from the magazine Psychology Today, by Nigel Barber, PH.D. titled: "Why Liberal Hearts Bleed and Conservatives Don't"

"Conservatives see the world as a challenging place in which there is always someone else who is ready to steal your lunch. Confronted by a potentially hostile environment, the best course is to take precautions and to ensure your own well being and that of your family."
"The threatening world view illuminates the conservative take on specific political issues in fairly obvious ways."
And he gives several examples, such as: "They fear attacks by other nations and therefore support a strong military and a bellicose foreign policy on the theory that a good attack is the best defense."

"Liberals take a more optimistic view of the world as being somewhat more benign." "They favor negotiation and consensus building over warfare in foreign policy and do not believe in excessive military buildups that drain social spending."

Let's look at a different article from Psychology Today, this one by Ronald E Riggio PH.D. titled "Liberals Can't Help It: Is Political Orientation Biologically Determined"

29

"Liberals are found to be more empathic, compassionate) (and open to experiences, while conservatives tend to be more concerned with order and preserving the existing social structure."

Let's look at an article dated 4/12/12 in the Washington Post written by Chris Mooney, author of "The Republican Brain: The Science of Why They Deny Science – and Reality"

Mooney discusses the factor attributed more to Republicans "The need for cognitive closure"

"This describes discomfort with uncertainty and a desire to resolve it into a firm belief. Someone with a high need for closure tends to seize on a piece of information that dispels doubt or ambiguity, and then freeze, refusing to consider new information. Those who have this trait can also be expected to spend less time processing information than those who are driven by different motivations, such as achieving accuracy." This finding is helpful when we look at the political affiliations of the most educated people in our society, our University Professors and Reporters.

A September 2016 edition of Econ Journal Watch did a study of political affiliation at 40 leading Universities and found that among our educators, the Professors, Democrats outnumbered Republicans by a ratio of 11 ½ to 1. Similarly, or even more striking, a 5/6/14 report by the Washington Post found that among reporters – those whose job is to see the world as it is and to report on it accurately, only 7% were Republicans.

Finally, let's look at a study by Peter John Loewen, Christopher Cochrane, and Gabriel Arsenault titled "Empathy and Political Preferences" from the University of Toronto.

"We argue that empathy exercises an influence over political preferences in a consistent and theoretically informed way. We present findings indicating that individuals who have a greater empathic capacity are more likely to identify with parties of the left." "As we show, partisanship varies systematically with the individual difference of empathy." "more generally, leaders of the left are usually perceived as more empathic and caring (Goren, 2005; Hayes,2005). Graham and Haidt's Moral Foundations Theory (Graham, Haidt and Nosek, 2009) similarly contends that "caring" is more central to the moral system of the left than the right.

Now, let's put the icing on the cake. This time I am going to quote from a piece written by Weissbourd and Jones of the Making Caring Common Project, Harvard Graduate School of Education. The piece is titled: "How Parents Can Cultivate Empathy In Children":

"Empathy is at the heart of what it means to be human. It's a foundation for acting ethically, for good relationships of many kinds, for loving well, and for professional success."

So that concludes my discussion on conservatism which is embodied by the very conservative American Enterprise Institute which has some board members who are also CFR members. Now let's look at the Peterson Institute.

The Peterson Institute includes 20 CFR members on its 43 member board of directors. They state that they have "helped provide the intellectual foundation for many of the major international financial initiatives of the past three decades." In other words, their work has contributed to the growth of widespread poverty around the world.

When economists note that overall numbers of extreme poor have decreased on a worldwide basis, they include

China in order to be able to make that statement. But China follows a different economic policy than that prescribed by the IMF and WTO, and China's huge success over the last 3 decades has moved so many Chinese people out of poverty that the overall world statistics can show an overall improvement. Taking China out of the equation, we can measure the neoliberal economic policy prescription, which is prescribed by U.S. Foreign Policy and the CFR, and this accounts for a large increase in world poverty.

Not only have the economic policies of the CFR contributed to the increase of global poverty. Those same policies have been followed, since the Reagan presidency, by both the Republican and the Democratic parties. Neoliberal financial policies are designed to increase the wealth and income of Capital.

This subject – an increase in world poverty, will be pursued in greater detail later in this book.

I will now follow up with a description of some of the domestic results of these types of policies.

- Higher education is increasingly no longer affordable for the average American, and is now mostly reserved for students from wealthy families. According to a report from the Experian Reporting Agency, student debt has now accumulated to 1.41 trillion dollars, which is more than all of the credit card debt combined in the U.S. This debt is now, due to changes in the law, no longer cancellable in bankruptcy.

- A large number of Americans, 57% cannot afford a $500.00 emergency without having to borrow, according to CBS News.

- Public Water Systems are emitting an unsafe level of lead into drinking water, and money to replace old disintegrating lead pipes is nowhere to be found. The American Society of Civil Engineers in a 2017 report noted that one million miles of pipes, which provide drinking water to 18 million people need to be replaced and that it will cost one trillion dollars to do so.

- The American Society of Civil Engineers also notes that the U.S. needs to find 2 trillion dollars to repair our infrastructure over the next two decades. Failing to act to rebuild America's infrastructure costs every American family $3,400.00 per year with very significant costs to the nation as a whole. A report was generated titled: "2017 Infrastructure Report Card". Infrastructure in this report covers Parks, Sold Waste treatment, Waste Water, Transit, Inland Water Ways Rail, Schools, Hazardous Waste, Aviation, Bridges, Dams, Drinking Water, Energy, Roads, Ports and Levees (remember what happened to New Orleans with Katrina).

- As of 2019, more than 18 million households are using food stamps in order to ensure that there will be enough food to eat, although the Republicans have a plan to remove a large number of people from being eligible for the food stamp program.

- While the U.S. is spending about half of the combined world total spending on "defense", the U.S. government is deeply in debt, a situation that is projected to worsen over time. The following is from Wikipedia.org: As of 12/31/18 debt held by the public was 16.1 trillion, and intragovernmental holdings were 5.87 trillion, for a total of 21.97 trillion dollars, which amounts to 77% of GDP.

This large amount of debt can potentially lower the government's ability to respond to problems – for example, rebuilding our infrastructure - an investment in America's future. The risk of a financial crisis is also increased.

- Analysts have explained that Globalization is a good thing, but that semi-skilled American workers will be hit hard with lower wages. Fine, but semi-skilled workers – those with no college degree, make up 73% of the U.S. population, and that figure will increase, since the cost of education has now skyrocketed.

- Another problem caused by our current post-Reagan economic policies has to do with the financialization of the American economy. An article in Forbes magazine, dated 2/14/15 titled: "Wall Street and the Financialization of the Economy" notes that the growing scale and profitability of the Finance sector has occurred at the expense of the rest of the economy - as a result of deregulation. Most of its returns go to the wealthy, causing increased inequality.

With the growth of the Finance industry, we see an increase in financial risk.
In 1970 the Finance sector was 10% of the economy. By 2010 it had grown to 20% of the economy. The Finance sector does not create wealth like other sectors, such as farming, mining and manufacturing. In other words, it does not make anything, and speculating by banks bids up

34

the price on real estate and commodities – like food for example.

Wallstreet profits rose from just under 10% of the economy in 1982 to 40% of all corporate profits in 2003. Since 1980 the Finance industry has focused on short term profits over long term goals, creating a more fragile, hollowed out American economy.

- Many have referred to a problem with corporate governance, citing the short term profit model. Note that before the 1980's corporations very rarely repurchased their own stock, but from between 2010 to 2019 under a climate of deregulation, corporations have spent more money buying their own stock than they have spent on all other investments. In that ten year period, corporations have spent a total of 3.8 trillion dollars buying back their own stock.

Fortuna Advisors, a research company, found that 5 year afterwards, stocks of companies engaged in buybacks performed worse for shareholders than stocks of companies that did not buy back their own stock. Company managers who are paid with stock options do very well though. The SEC performed a study which revealed that eight days following a buy back announcement, executives on average sold five times as much of their company stock than they had on any other normal day. Critics have expressed the view that this type of behavior is a drain on Capital, which ultimately threatens the competitive prospects of American industry.

A CNN report dated 9/17/18 is titled as follows: "Corporate America is Spending More on Buybacks than Anything Else". CNN noted that according to Goldman Sachs, that in 19 out of the past 20 years, the number one use of funds by S & P companies is stock buybacks, more than investment in company expansion, more than research and development.

A fortune magazine article dated 8/20/19 is titled: "More Than Half of All Stock Buybacks are Now Financed by Debt'. Here's why that is a problem. The article, among other things, noted that "Buybacks are a strong catalyst for the Bull Market. In fact, they are a more significant factor than economic growth. A study last year in the Financial Analysts Journal noted that "the research covered 43 nations over two decades." In 2018, according to a study by Yardeni Research, borrowing funded 56% of that year's corporate stock buy backs.

Economists Piketty and Saez compiled a study in 2016 that shows that in 1980, the top 1% took home 8% of all revenue in the United States. Since 1980 an upward trend stops in 2015, at the study's end, and at this point the top 1% is taking home just over 18% of all income, more than a 100% increase. Economist Dean Baker reflected on this data, that this increased amount to the 1%, if redirected to everybody in the bottom 90%, would result in an increase in income of more than 20% for everybody else! So this upward trend for the 1%, those people who are already wealthy, has a very significant impact on the entire U.S. population.

The next subject we need to look at is the existential threat of an accidental nuclear war, and how the Council of Foreign Relations and the U.S. Foreign Policy regime has contributed to this – yet another existential threat.

The Council has supported the advance of NATO up to the doorstep of Russia, a country that has nuclear weapons. They also support how the U.S. has, over the years, built approximately 800 military bases outside the United States borders – a highly aggressive stance to take.

What are the chances of an accidental nuclear war that would end mankind?

. The Union of Concerned Scientists reported on their website that on 11/9/79 a Norad technician had accidently inserted a training tape into their operational Norad computer. The training tape simulated an attack from Russia. The Pentagon went on high alert, but just before the start of World War III, they were able to determine that it was a false alarm.

"Marshal Shulman, a senior state department advisor, would later note that "false alerts of this kind are not a rare occurrence."

However, If one were to google: List of Nuclear Close Calls, one comes upon an article by Wikipedia which has a summary line on close call incidents:

1950's: 11/5/56

1960's: 10/5/60, 11/24/61, 10/27/62, 11/9/65, 5/23/67

1970's: 11/9/79

1980's: 3/15/80, 9/26/83

1990's: 1/25/95

2010's: 10/23/2010

The Huffington Post came out with an article "The Top 10 Reasons to Reduce the Risk of Accidental Nuclear War". I will quote from that article:

"What's the number one military threat to the U.S.?

1   Terrorism
2   A deliberate nuclear attack
3   Accidental nuclear war with Russia

Based on the recent political debates, you'd think it would be 1 or 2, but if you do the numbers, 3 wins hands down."

Eric Schlosser wrote an excellent book titled "Command and Control". It reads like a great novel, and at the same time is the result of a great deal of first-rate investigative reporting about our nuclear weapons program. It even includes an historical perspective as well. This is an excellent book for those who wish to gain important understandings about the nuclear weapons subject matter.

Here are some quotes:

Referring to an interview with a retired Strategic Command General:

"And like almost every single Air Force Officer, Weapon Designer, Pentagon Official, Airman and Missile Maintenance Crew member whom I interviewed about the Cold War, he was amazed that nuclear weapons were never used, that no major city was destroyed, that the tiger never got loose."

A study by the Sandia Nuclear Weapons Lab found that from 1950 to 1968, at least 1,200 nuclear weapons had been involved in what they referred to as significant incidents and accidents. The official list of nuclear accidents compiled by the Department of Defense included 13 instances categorized by either an unauthorized launch or jettison of a weapon, a fire, an explosion, or a release of radioactivity. By 1968 at least 70 missiles with nuclear warheads had been involved in lightning accidents. Four nuclear missiles in Italy were struck by lightning. Some of their thermal batteries fired, and in two of the warheads, tritium gas was released, making them ready to produce nuclear explosions.

In Russia,

In 1983 a Soviet early warning satellite had detected five missiles approaching from the United States. Alarms went off in the air defense facility south of Moscow. Lieutenant Colonel Stanislav Petrov decided that it must have been a false alarm because only five missiles were detected. Surely a first strike attack would have had many more than that. It turns out, of course, that he was right. Their alarm had been triggered by rays of sunlight reflected off clouds. Thankfully, he had not communicated the need for a retaliation to his central command.

On 1/25/95, Norway launched a weather research rocket to study the aurora borealis. In spite of advanced warning to Russia about this launch, the Kremlin thought that they might be under attack from the United States. They went on full nuclear alert. Boris Yeltsin got as far as retrieving his launch codes, when it was finally determined to be a false alarm.

In the U.S.:

twice at Barksdale, a cart collapsed while transporting a launcher full of short-range nuclear bombs. Both times telescoping arms broke, dropping the bombs about five feet to the ground. At least two warheads and 6 missiles were damaged.

From Command and Control:

"At Carswell Air Force Base, someone on a loading crew had ignored a tech order and pulled a handle too hard in the cockpit of a B-52. Instead of opening the bomb bay doors, he'd inadvertently released a b-61 hydrogen bomb. It fell about seven feet and hit the runway."

In 2013 the Defense Science board explained that the vulnerability of their systems to cyberattack had not been fully studied.

With all of this history, one might wonder about the wisdom or lack thereof, of surrounding Russia with short range nuclear missile sites all pointed at Russia, with Russia fully aware of this. One might wonder about the wisdom, or lack thereof, of deciding to spend 1.2 billion dollars over the next ten years to make smaller nuclear bombs so that the unthinkable becomes thinkable - to use them.

We truly cannot afford to take the current approaches and positions that we are taking in our nation's foreign policy. One obvious and simple solutions would be to must accept the sovereignty of all foreign nations. That would be the moral, ethical approach. It is time that our "Department of Defense" be re made to be just that – for defense only. The U.S. currently has approximately five thousand military bases located inside the country. Even that is too many. The last time that the U.S. was attacked was during the war of 1812, and even that was never meant to be more than a show of force vs a full scale invasion.

Business people, in their depravity, want to use the power and resources of the U.S. government to take what belongs to other people under a veil of "National Security", but in fact, in too many cases, our foreign policy is the exact opposite of National Security. The effects of this immoral stance that our government takes can be seen not only in our inner cities, but increasingly in every level of American society.

It is easy to see how since Reagan, the Council on Foreign Relations and their class have damaged the American economy and the world economy, endangering and damaging the lives of hundreds of millions of people. The methodology by which this comes to pass will be explained in detail in the discussion of their article concerning "Why Latin America Was Primed to Explode". The workings of the World Trade Organization will be explored.

It is also clear that our government has promoted a game of "chicken", or atomic Russian Roulette with Russia, playing with the future of mankind.

It is also clear that they have put the question of human survival into question with their approach to global warming, and it is also clear that their actions have generated a worldwide hurricane of turmoil and war around the world, with their over throw of so many foreign leaders, and the invasion of Iraq and other nations.

I found many of the articles in Foreign Affairs magazine to be truly shocking, and I will now walk through some of these articles and look at what I found to be problematic. Articles in Foreign Affairs can be quite interesting, because so many of their positions are easily demonstrated to be contrary to verifiable facts. They aren't stupid, which means that they tow whatever line means money for their group. And the rich indeed get richer.

This group is not capable of changing based on its own internal dynamics. Outside energy is needed in order to change this equation. The general public needs to become more educated in these matters and to form a political force for change.

Chapter 2

"Why Latin America Was Primed to Explode – Economic Malaise, More than foreign meddling, explains the outpouring of rage. 10-29-19 by Moises Naim and Brian Winter, Foreign Affairs Magazine.

This article discusses the recent wave of massive protests all around South America, and allegations of foreign meddling as a possible cause of the protests. The article then concludes that it is more than foreign meddling which has caused the protests. The article explains that the cause of the turmoil is not foreign meddling, but is in fact economic malaise.

Quoted from the article: "On the one hand, their constituents demand that they take immediate, sweeping action to fix problems that in many cases have festered for decades, if not centuries."

In the following pages I will explain what that problem is which has been festering for decades, and I will show that this economic malaise is indeed being caused by foreign meddling. The article points to Cuba and Venezuela as the would-be meddlers and then dismisses it as not significant enough to cause millions of people to take to the streets in protest. The article dismisses foreign meddling as a reason for the widescale protests in Latin America, but I disagree with the analysis and point to the United States as in fact the foreign meddler and the cause of the torment.

There are three organizations that the United States uses, along with its European allies, to expropriate the property of foreign nations in a way that appears on the surface to be legitimate, but which in fact denies foreign nations their own sovereignty. These methodologies succeed based on the desperation of many government leaders in third world countries, and also because governments of third world countries do not have the means to be assisted with large teams of lawyers and trade experts. Those organizations are the World Trade Organization, the World Bank, and the International Monetary Fund. Through these supposedly legitimate neutral multi-lateral organizations, the terms of trade are directed in favor of the advanced nations, to the detriment of the developing, or, third world countries.

When discussing problems in Latin America, would it be relevant to explain how the United States and Europe have prevented Latin America from achieving economic development? I believe so.

The World Trade Organization was developed out of an earlier treaty called the General Agreement on Tariffs and Trade, or GATT. The rules were developed by an association between the U.S. Government and 500 Multi-National Corporations designated as formal U.S. Government advisers, who crafted a treaty that would benefit them but unfortunately, as it turns out, at the expense of third world developing nations such as those found in Latin America, and all other entities that do not go by the description of Multi-National Corporations.

The U.S. general public is also included as victims of these organizations. Note the effects of "globalization" on the U.S. Manufacturing sector, and on the job market in general. And the United States government was mainly responsible for the creation, promotion and implementation of the WTO.

Public services, democratically managed, are the principal means for guaranteeing citizen wide access to education, health care, water, roads, sanitation, food security, physical security and a safety net for those in need. Among other things, the WTO was created to turn these fundamental services into commodities to become new private business opportunities, taking them out of public control.

The WTO seeks to restrain governments' rights to regulate in the service sector. The WTO threatens public access to what are basic public services. Disguised under the rubric of trade, we find a corporate coup d'etat of the State. The WTO rules allow public services of member states to become privatized, but forbids member governments from taking back control of such services, once they have become privatized.

The World Trade Organization, or the WTO, was promoted to the third world as a vehicle for trade that would be economically beneficial to them. Although the treaty has been very beneficial to multi-national corporations from the developed countries, it has been a disaster for Latin America and the Third World. A strong correlation exists between the implementation of the WTO and a sharp increase in extreme poverty in Latin America, and throughout the Third World.

Leaving China out of the equation, the number of people living on less than $2 per day, outside China, rose from 1.9 billion in 1990 to 2.2 billion in 1999, and this happened despite overall global economic growth. How did this happen?

The rules of the World Trade Organization require countries to indiscriminately lower their barriers to trade and capital, leaving the smaller nations wide open for foreign takeover of their entire economies. No country has ever developed under those types of conditions and rules that have been codified by the WTO.

This subject is reviewed quite thoroughly by Economist Ha Joon Chang, assistant Director of Development Studies at Cambridge University, as well as by Economist Joseph Stiglitz, a Nobel Prize winner in Economics. I highly recommend the book "Whose Trade Organization?" by Lori Wallach and Patrick Woodall, as well as "Unholy Trinity" by Professor Richard Peet. Economist and Professor Michael Hudson is also an important resource for this subject matter. Noam Chomsky, and many others, have written about this subject matter at great length.

Developing countries need to be able to choose their own policies in order to develop their own industries over time, to a certain level before choosing, if they dare, to compete on a worldwide level. The WTO employs a one size fits all model. In matters of trade, such an approach only works to the benefit of all parties when the agreement is between countries that have the same level of economic and technical development. The WTO is designed so that advanced countries will dominate the developing countries, and, in fact, that is the result of these policies.

UNCTAD, the United Nations Conference on Trade & Development reported that since the WTO's implementation the least developed countries, LDC, who followed the strictures of the WTO by reducing their trade barriers the most, had higher extreme poverty **increases** than the LDC's who reduced their trade barriers the least,.

The rules of the WTO are an attack on governance and democracy. For example, a WTO dispute panel in January 1996 ruled that the U.S. Clean Air Act regulations were a violation of trade rules. The WTO went into effect on January 1, 1995. Since the book "Whose Trade Organization?" was published by the organization Public Citizen in 2004 (by Lori Wallach and Patrick Woodall), they noted: "Since it was created in 1995, the WTO has ruled that **every** environmental, health or safety policy it has reviewed **but one** is an illegal trade barrier that must be eliminated or changed", and also, "panels have ruled against **all** food-safety regulations under review on the grounds that they restrict trade more than necessary." (my emphasis added). The WTO had also as of 2004 ruled against **every** effort to prevent the entry of agricultural pests and other invasive species between countries engaged in trade.

WTO rules forbid export limits that are designed to prevent depletion of natural resources from mines, forests and fisheries.

In order to have sustainable management of coastal fisheries, governments must be able to impose controls on catches. Under WTO rules, controls are considered a "non-trade tariff barrier" and are therefore not permitted!

If a government that is a WTO member disagrees with a WTO ruling and proceeds to violate the ruling by banning or regulating a certain practice, they can be sued by private companies and ordered to pay private companies for revenues that the companies had anticipated they would have earned if the government had not banned or regulated the industry in question.

The WTO uses the subject of Trade to subvert governments, which devastates Latin America, along with the rest of the world. WTO agricultural rules allowed the countries that had subsidies in place at the time the WTO started, the advanced countries, to maintain them, including export subsidies which benefit agribusiness corporations. Poorer countries did not have such subsidies at the time and under the WTO rules, are not now allowed to implement them if they did not have them before. This ruling also encourages third world farmers to engage in the production of more lucrative crops instead, such as Opium poppy and Coca, for cocaine production.

The WTO rules require that there will be no restrictions on the part of any country, on imported agricultural products, resulting in U.S. and European government subsidized agricultural products being able to under sell the products in other countries and to put farmers out of business in third world countries, causing them to move to cities, looking for non-existent jobs and creating shanty towns in the process. This is what has happened all around the world. This also results in increased importation of foods by developing countries. This causes food insecurity on national levels in these countries and also creates national trade imbalances.

The book "Trade for Life" by Mark Curtis noted the following: "As a group, the least developed countries have changed from being relatively self-sufficient to being net food importers – what the Secretary General of UNCTAD, Rubens Ricuperto, has described as "one of the darkest stories of the last 25 years".

One well known example is that NAFTA put more than 2 million Mexican corn farmers out of business! Because of U.S. government subsidies paid to farmers, U.S. corn cost less in Mexico than what it costs Mexican farmers in Mexico to produce. So many Mexican corn farmers have been put out of business as a result. This has caused national food insecurity in Mexico (and elsewhere).

The Mexican Institute of Social Security has stated that one result of the NAFTA treaty is that 158,000 Mexican children die each year before reaching the age of five due to illnesses contracted as a result of malnutrition. In another example of food insecurity, A 1996 corn shortage

48

in the U.S. resulted in malnourishment of 20% of all of the children in Mexico.

The over production and exporting of government subsidized agricultural products world-wide from advanced countries, has caused a crash in commodities prices, which the WTO rules have ensured. The IMF and World Bank have asked developing countries to increase commodity production for export in order to earn hard currency to repay their loans, but with all of these countries doing the same, over supply is created, resulting in lower prices for their products on the world market. Commodity agreements regulating supply and pricing that had been in effect in the past under GAAT were eliminated. Poverty on a world level is rising because of these policies pushed by the U.S. and Europe through the WTO. A good book on this subject would be "The Globalization of Poverty" by Canadian economist Michel Chussodovsky.

Regarding Third World debt, John Perkins, author of "Confessions of an Economic Hit Man" writes extensively about corporations that work with the U.S. government and solicit huge over-sized infrastructure projects aimed at chaining third world countries to debt dependency with Western Banks. Here is a quote from an article titled: "In Hock to Uncle Sam" from the Guardian, dated 1/28/06:

John Perkins was recruited as a young man by the National Security Agency - somewhat to his surprise, considering that in his interview he had been grilled on his youthful insubordination, friendships with suspicious foreigners, and sexual frustrations. It turns out that it doesn't hurt to be a bit damaged in the NSA's eyes - it makes you more biddable. He was then employed by Chas T Main, a company whose competitors included Bechtel and Halliburton, of which you may have heard. As to what Main's business was, Perkins says that "during my first months there even I could not figure out what we did".

He found out eventually. Ostensibly an economist, his job was to go off to developing countries, offer them enormous loans with which to improve their infrastructures, and provide wildly inflated projections of the economic growth these improvements would bring. Presented to the right people, these bogus figures did the trick, a deliberately underhand assault on a nation's de facto sovereignty. Contractors - US contractors, naturally - would move in and build the pipelines or the drilling platforms or the power stations, the economy would fail to grow anything like as fast as predicted, the country would default on its loan, and so find itself in hock to the US in perpetuity - or until it underwent revolutionary regime change.

The following is a quote from John Perkins himself, expressed in an article from Monthly Review, dated 3/1/13 titled: "Rise of the Corporatocracy: An Interview with John Perkins"

"Economic hit men (EHMs) are highly paid professionals who cheat countries around the globe out of trillions of dollars. They funnel money from the World Bank, the U.S. Agency for International Development (USAID), and other foreign "aid" organizations into the coffers of huge corporations and the pockets of a few wealthy families who control the planet's natural resources. Their tools include fraudulent financial reports, rigged elections, payoffs, extortion, sex, and murder. They play a game as old as empire, but one that has taken on new and terrifying dimensions during this time of globalization. I should know; I was an EHM."

Third world countries were recovering from centuries of exploitation by European powers, and third world economies were experiencing a steady 3% rate of economic growth, using import substitution and other methods for their development. They were taking out short term loans from U.S. banks in this process, however, starting in 1979, Paul Volker, the Chairman of a private banking organization confusingly called the Federal Reserve, raised interest rates through 1981, up to 21.5%.

This was the beginning of disaster for Third World countries, who have re paid the principle many times over in the process of meeting the interest payments, and considering the level of poverty in the third world, this is blood money. It was then in the early 80's that the IMF began its "Structural Adjustment" programs which made it impossible for third world governments to be able to accumulate enough funds to ever pay off their debts.

Because of the WTO agreements and the monopolization of agricultural trade by a handful of Agribusiness giants, trans-national Agribusiness companies are able to negotiate down the prices paid to farmers, playing off pricing from farmers from different countries against one another. The four Agribusiness giants are able to manipulate prices by hoarding agricultural products and then releasing them for sale and flooding the market at harvest time, thus crashing the prices at the time that the new harvests are ready to go to market. Then these same companies buy up the new harvests at fire sale prices.

The crash in prices paid to farmers is a windfall for the small handful of multi-national agribusiness companies, and because the distribution market is monopolized, food prices to consumers go up instead of down. For example, food prices in the U.S. for food eaten at home by consumers rose by 32% between 1994 to 2002 under the auspices of the WTO agreements in trade.

By 2002, the largest six agribusiness companies that deal with grain, controlled 75% of the world's cereal commodity market. (Grain and Milling Annual Report, 2002: Mary Hendrickson and William Heffernan, Dept. of Rural Sociology, Univ of Missouri "Concentration of Agricultural Markets" Feb 2002).According to an article from the Guardian dated 6/21/2011, titled: "The Global Food Crisis: ABCD of Food – how the Multi-Nationals Dominate Trade", only 4 agribusiness giants control between 75% to 90% of the world grain market.

So the happy news is that these trade agreements provide increased opportunities for American companies. The sad part is all the children who must die in the process. According to a 2018 study by Unicef – the United Nations agency, 3.1 million children die every year from malnutrition. Malnutrition is not due to actual literal food shortages but is instead due to a lack of the ability of many to pay for the food.

According to the USDA's Economic Research Service, farm debt in the U.S. has risen steadily since the WTO went into effect. Also, Malnutrition is an enormous problem in the third world, and it is intimately intertwined with the WTO's treatment of food as a tradeable commodity instead of as the basis of life. On a Democracy Now broadcast on 11/27/19, Vandana Shiva, a scholar, a physicist and environmental activist reported that approximately 500,000 farmers in India have committed suicide because of unpayable debt they incurred in the process of adopting the use of seeds and pesticides from Western corporations under the trade rule regime of the WTO. Lori Wallach, co-author of Whose Trade Organization? was also a part of that same broadcast. Based on their discussion on Democracy Now, it seems that not much if anything has changed since the initial publication of that extremely important book, "Whose Trade Organization?"

It is my guess that the U.S. government allowed monopolies to re-develop and become an integral part of the U.S. economy because they can be used as a tool for absolute control over a population or populations – especially in the case of the Multi-National corporation. Perhaps this would be part of a totalitarian or militaristic strategy. If that is the case, then it would be my belief that the U.S. government will have the power also - to change this.

The WTO operates in secret. Their text is written in trade language and the WTO does not translate their documents into other languages. So in part, Latin American nations have to rely on their belief in the good will of the United States Government.

It is surmised that although many developing countries disagree with the agricultural policies and many of the other policies, that the package is presented on an all or nothing basis, where the negotiators from third world countries have to put their hopes in future negotiations.

Negotiations in the WTO are only held between developed Western nations, behind closed doors, and third world nations are not allowed at the negotiating table, and there is no public access to their decision-making processes.

Developing countries do not have the money or expertise to bring cases to the WTO nor to defend themselves against challenges to their government policies brought before them through the WTO.

In terms of labor and environmental standards the WTO promotes "huckster capitalism" and a race to the bottom. For example, under WTO rules, manufacturers are not required to prove that a product is safe before it can be sold. Instead, governments must prove that a product is unsafe before they can ban it. Member nations may not take any precautionary measures in deciding whether to allow or disallow the importation of any product, without being able to provide exact scientific proof of harm. They would have to be able to first prove exactly how much harm would be caused by the product in question – that is, they must be able to quantify the damage that would be caused by the product.

WTO food safety standards allow for residues of pesticides that have been banned in the United States. For example, DDT residue is allowed in milk, meat and grain. In some cases, pesticide residues are permitted at five times the legal limit in the U.S as of the 2004 publication of "Whose Trade Organization?"

The WTO is surrounded with lies.

The International Organization for Standardization, or ISO is a private body that works with the WTO to set standards for non-food products. The "ISO 14000 series" set standards for environmental management practices and they have a "best environmental practice" seal. However, a company is not required to meet any particular performance standards in order to obtain this seal!!

The WTO noted that WTO members are free to set their own environmental objectives, *but only through measures that are consistent with the WTO.*

There is a clause in a preamble stating that the WTO recognizes governments' rights to regulate in the service sector, but the actual rules set numerous restrictions on the ways that governments can regulate services in their respective countries.

Countries can have policies necessary to protect public morals, maintain public order, protect human, animal and plant life or health, *"which are not inconsistent with the provisions of GATS"*

Note that the U.S. and European governments touted a study from the OEDC and the World Bank which concluded that the world income would grow by 213 billion dollars per year if the Uruguay round (an earlier incarnation of the WTO) were implemented. This report actually concluded that this would happen **starting in the tenth year** after implementation – meaning only a 0.7% per year growth rate! (Ian Golden, Odin Knudsen and Dominique van der Mensbrugghe, Trade Liberalization: Global Economic Implications (Washington, D.C.: World Bank 1993) at 13). Curiously, main stream media failed to report on this very important distinction being made.

As a U.S. Trade Representative, Robert Zoellick, a notable council member on the Council of Foreign Relations, in promoting the WTO, had stated that "between 1990 and 2000, that "exports of goods and services have accounted for one-fifth of U.S. economic growth." What he did not mention was that during that same period, imports had increased to such an extent that the trade deficit had grown to five times larger than it had been as of the first day of the WTO's implementation, and imports represent a drag on the economy because of jobs lost. Maybe just an oversight on his part? So yes, the exports resulted in growth, but the imports resulted in exactly the opposite, and the imports were much greater than the exports, but Zoellick proved to be a rather unreliable spokesman, although he was a U.S. Trade Representative, as he mis characterized, or, shall we say, lied about the data.

One study by World Bank economist David Dollar and Aart Kray explains that more open countries have the highest growth rates. The study mentions a long known fact that increased growth rates can lead to poverty reduction. Then the study goes on to **assume** that trade liberalization causes economic growth, in spite of the fact that empirical data proves just exactly the opposite of their statement.

China's strong economic growth over the last few decades is included in the study to prove his point. Because of its huge population, China weighed heavily in this analysis, however China has broad restrictions on imports and foreign investment, and China, it turns out, is a Communist country. It does not follow the usual WTO prescriptions.

In promoting the WTO, The Economic Policy Institute, a Washington Think Tank found that U.S. export growth between 1994 and 2000 created 2.7 million jobs. True, but what they didn't notice was that faster **import** growth had eliminated 5.8 million jobs. Maybe that is just another oversight?

I asked the organization Public Citizen why countries are not simply leaving the WTO. I had surmised on my part, that there would be many leaders who would fear being on the wrong end of a U.S. sponsored Coup d'etat if they left. Here is the response from Public Citizen:

"Here are some reasons I've found that countries don't leave the WTO and create alternatives:

- The Bretton Woods organizations and related organizations really work together. So, leaving the WTO could negatively impact countries' abilities to qualify for World Bank/IMF assistance, for example

- The politically powerful people that committed countries to the WTO within each country are quite often the wealthiest in each country and have strong ties to multinational corporations. So, those countries' WTO commitments don't represent the interest of the people, and it is hard to pull out because of internal power dynamics within each country
- A lot of multinational corporations' investment is contingent upon participating in WTO-style trade liberalization. Politicians in those countries feel beholden to serve the corporations to ensure continued inbound investment, even if that investment isn't adequately benefiting the country (or even harming it)
- There is still a pervasive ideological bent towards unbridled free trade as a good thing by definition – and that is hard to change. Many people in both advanced and developing countries think of the WTO as a net good.
- Because the WTO creates a race-to-the-bottom in terms of regulatory, safety, and labor standards, a developing country may find it difficult to keep standards high in the face of so much competition and political pressure.

There is something called the "WTO turnaround agenda", which is an active movement of working people around the world to create an alternative to the WTO. "

Trade analysts with a focus on developing countries and economic development wrote an account of gross manipulation and dirty tricks that the WTO applies to developing nations at their meetings, so that the advanced countries can have their way in the negotiations. In the book titled "Behind the Scenes at the WTO" by Fatoumata Jawara and Aileen Kwa;

The Cancun meeting of the WTO is discussed. The European Communities (EC) trade commissioner, Pascal Lamy is quoted: "Delegation after delegation took the floor to denounce the text as a travesty of justice, as an affront to every developing country, as a heresy of enormous magnitude."

The trade representative from India stated:

"We have to express our disappointment that the revised text brought out by you has arbitrarily disregarded views and concerns expressed by us. We wonder now whether development here refers to only further development of the developed countries."

An African negotiator had explained that the Kenyan Minister, who was the chair of the Development Working Group, was presented with a report by the WTO Secretariat that summarized the results of his consultations which he himself did not prepare. He was given some notes to read which said that the report was ready, but he, the Chair of that group, had not even seen this report.

The WTO Secretariat, after the Cancun meetings, distributed a letter from the IMF and World Bank which promised loans to countries willing to show flexibility to re start the negotiations. One African official stated: "why should I lose revenue that I now collect (by reducing tariffs), and be given a loan?" " it doesn't make sense." "what can we use to repay the loans if there is no revenue to collect?" "This organization is crazy!"

Yet, there is a rationale. When the IMF gives a loan to a country, the loan comes with conditions. The conditions are that the nation receiving the loan must open up their country to foreign investment and free trade, and drop movement of capital restrictions, thus insuring that their economy gets taken over by giant foreign multi-national corporations. Government services and industries are to be privatized, thus depriving governments of sources of needed funds. The weakening of foreign governments means the strengthening of Multi-National corporations, under the WTO agreements.

In the Seattle & Doha WTO meetings which were in years prior to the Cancun meeting, drafts of the WTO declaration were available six to eight weeks prior to the meetings. Then for the Cancun meetings, WTO declarations were not made available until two weeks before the meeting. The authors of the book "Behind the Scenes at the WTO" expressed their view that this was a deliberate effort to silence discussion and create a situation which would result in further submission to the WTO's position from the Developing countries. Once the drafts became available, they expressed U.S. and European positions. The General Council then declared that the text would not be amended.

One official from a developing country stated: "All that we fought for in the last eighteen months has been coolly set aside. They released (the draft) in the evening on Sunday after we had met for the whole day. At the end of a whole day's discussion, they say, "Here is the text!" They were wasting our time!" "Then they give us no time to assess the text because they convened an informal meeting on Monday afternoon. On Monday after all the delegations had completed making their statements, the Chair announces that the formal General Council meetings will be held the next day, so please don't repeat yourself....So they ensure that people let off steam in the informal (off the record) meeting, so that in the formal (on the record) meeting there would be less opposition".

The text was very strong on eliminating agricultural tariffs for developing countries, but reproduced the American and European positions and actually gave the developed countries increased abilities to hide farm subsidies without having to lessen or relinquish them. On the industrial side, the authors expressed the view that the formula on cutting industrial tariffs represented "A sure road towards the destruction of developing counties' industries."

This was only a small sample of what that book uncovers, again: "Behind the Scenes at the WTO".

The IMF, or International Monetary Fund is largely controlled by the United States Treasury.

The IMF grants loans to countries only if the borrowing country will follow their plan. The plan is the same for all nations. It favors quick repayment to the bank, but it also sets up the borrowing country to end up having a very weak government and a very poor population. The winners are the multi-national corporations who are able to come in and buy up the more productive elements of these third world nations. So the conditions tied to loans from the International Monetary Fund in the long run end up providing massive investment opportunities for first world countries' corporations and banks, into third world countries, impoverishing the multitudes of people who live in the third world countries in the process.

The following conditions must be followed:

Third world nations must remove their trade tariff barriers and therefore compete head on with the developed world immediately.

Although, the economic history of the developed world demonstrates that trade barriers were always used in the form of tariffs so that the local industries would be protected against foreign competition. In this way, local industries were able to develop over time. Only in the mid-1800's, for example, did England attempt a period of "free trade", but that was because they were very far ahead of the rest of the world in manufacturing, so they could afford "free trade" knowing that they would be the winners.

The position taken by the WTO, IMF and World Bank, is that third world nations must allow foreign capital free reign to invest or divest, and to move funds in or out of the country with little or no restrictions. This is called "Capital Account Liberalization."

Economist Joseph Stiglitz wrote that this Capital Account Liberalization policy was the number 1 cause of the East Asian financial crash of the 1990's. It introduces the possibility of currency speculation, which can be deadly for smaller nations enmeshed in globalization, who have no way of protecting themselves from giant western banks who in many cases have more funds to play with than do entire small nations, and who are very strongly in the business of speculation.

Another issue is the devaluation of currency that happens in the international markets under the circumstances that allow the free movement of capital. When a country has a loan that is denominated in U.S. dollars, and then their currency is now worth much less in international markets due to aggressive acts of currency speculation, now that country will no longer be able to pay back that U.S. dollar denominated loan anytime soon, and the IMF is there to cause even further damage by extending further loans with more conditions that will have to be met by the borrowing country.

The IMF has also asked countries to lower their currently exchange rate as a pre-condition for a loan. This means that the dollar denominated loan can never be repaid, unless something very unusual were to occur.

Third world nations are directed to raise their interest rates, supposedly to cool the economy and reduce inflation.

This results in a business slow down, because so much of business is run on credit, and so a great deal of unemployment is caused by this policy.

Third world countries must undergo an austerity plan whereby the government sector shrinks.

This approach causes unemployment among those who had previously been employed as government workers. It also shrinks the power of the government in question.

Third world countries' governments must cut many government services and subsidies, and this is referred to as an austerity plan. Instead, the government must concentrate on paying back the loan as soon as possible. No matter what.

Greece is an excellent recent example of these policies.

This is precisely what causes riots. Many among the poor feel that by removing the government subsidies on food and fuel, that the social contract is broken. The state's legitimacy comes into question when the price of necessities is now suddenly out of reach, and money and profit suddenly become more important than the lives of the poor.

This is why large numbers of people protest when their country obtains a loan from the IMF.

So these policies help the wealthy people from the developed nations to get richer, and the money comes directly from the poor people in the third world.

Third world countries' governments must sell off many of their services to private service providers. Typically, when governments sell off their own services, the pricing is substantially below the actual true value of such services. As an example, a government might sell a dam for 10% of what it had cost to build, providing a private electric company with a boon, while depriving the government of future revenues from the sale of the electricity.

Government provision of monopoly type services almost always results in the lowering of the cost of living for the general public, as it is so designed to do. The Government does not have advertising costs, they do not need to pay a C.E.O., nor a board of directors, the Government does not need to pay dividends to shareholders they don't need to pay corporate attorneys and tax accountants, and the Government does not retain a profit. How can private enterprise compete with that? The answer is - they can't.

That is why when a government privatizes any of their services, the general public is left either with having to pay higher prices or experience a reduction in the quality of service, or both.

With this explanation of the WTO and the IMF I would like to refer to Kimberly Clausing's article in this same publication, titled "The progressive case against protectionism". On page 120 of the discussed issue of Foreign Affairs magazine, she writes: "In the end, global markets have many wonderful benefits, but they need to be accompanied by strong domestic policies to ensure that the benefits of international trade (as well as technological change and other forces) are felt by all.

I completely agree with the author on that point, however, under the current trade regime, this is completely impossible. It would seem as though she is not aware of this, and due to all the secrecy, I am not surprised.

The World Bank is a sister organization, part of the three headed monster. **One condition that the World Bank has imposed on many third world countries is that they lower their currency exchange rate as a condition of the loan.** By lowering their exchange rate, their exports will be cheaper to first world countries which will tend to be a stimulus to export trade, however, with the terms of trade as such, they will have to experience a gigantic increase in exports in order to be able to repay their dollar denominated World Bank loan, **because now their currency is smaller than it was before, when compared with the dollar. So this type of approach will tend to lock in a country into eternal debt with the U.S.**

Many people write about this subject; Economist Ha Joon Chang of Cambridge University, Nobel Prize winning Economist Joseph Stiglitz, economist and Professor, Michael Hudson, Political Science PHD and Professor Michael Parenti, Professor Richard Peet, Mark Curtis, Professor Noam Chomsky, reporter, author Naomi Klein, Attorney Lori Wallach of Public Citizen, and many others.

An old joke in Latin America goes as follows: Why is there no Coups d'etat in the United States? Answer: Because there are no U.S. Embassies in the United States.

Below are but a few examples of foreign meddling, which the Foreign Affairs article states is not Latin America's problem:

Ecuador: On September 30, 2010 a Coup attempt was made against democratically elected president Rafael

Correa. The attempt was made by elements of the National Police in Quito. It was later found that these police were paid three times their normal salary by an outside government, the United States. The payments were made through the U.S. consulate office in Quito Ecuador. So this can be considered an example of foreign meddling that this article is talking about, although this example is not mentioned in the article.

Honduras: On June 28,2009, democratically elected president Manuel Zelaya was overthrown in a Coup.

The Organization of American States recognized this as a Coup. The European Union recognized this as a Coup, and the United Nations recognized this as Coup. However, strangely enough, the United States did not recognize this as a coup.

The United States, under Secretary of State Hillary Clinton, demanded or suggested that instead of re instating the duly elected President, that instead, they would have a quick snap election, and that Manuel Zelaya would not be allowed to run. So the government of Honduras followed suit and the United States offered their diplomatic support. In this way, Zelaya was "officially" overthrown.

This would be one other example of "foreign meddling" that the article discusses, although this example is not mentioned in the article. The new Honduran government is made up of drug runners and has destroyed the nation, as explained by Dana Frank in her book The Long Honduran Night. That would be an example of "turmoil" that the article talks about.

Bolivia: on March 9, 2009 a diplomat from a foreign country was ordered to leave the country because he was found to be conspiring with opposition groups. The foreign country was the United States. This would be an example of foreign meddling.

Prior to the last election of Evo Morales, Marco Rubio complained that the upcoming Bolivian election could end up with election irregularities. Less than a week before the October 20 election, Carlos Mesa was trailing Evo Morales with 22 percent against 38 percent for Morales. The final election result had Mesa with 37% and Morales 47%, so Morales, who was ahead by 17 percentage points ended up winning only one week later, by only ten percentage points. That is odd, but the irregularity pertains to the losing candidate, not to Evo Morales.

After the election, the Organization of American States complained about irregularities in the election, but absolutely no evidence whatsoever was presented.

The commander of Bolivia's armed forces, William Kaliman, executed the Coup. In the past, he had served as a military attaché at the Bolivian Embassy in Washington. During that time he was trained by what then was called the School of the Americas at a U.S. Military base in Ft Benning, Georgia. The Canadian reporting agency Global Research reported that immediately after the Coup, Kaliman left Bolivia for the United States and he had somehow acquired one million U.S. dollars from somewhere. Perhaps military positions in Bolivia pay quite well?

After the government was chased out of Bolivia, Jeanine Añez, an opposition senator, declared herself interim-President, and, the Constitutional Court confirmed the legality of the transfer of power even though her nomination was unconstitutional.

Yet in spite of all that, the United States **immediately** expressed their approval and diplomatic support of this illegal government that seized power by way of a military coup. This is called meddling.

Haiti: In 2004, democratically elected President Jean-Bertrand Aristide was overthrown in a Coup that his administration described as organized by a foreign government, the United States. An armed group entered Haiti through the Dominican Republic. This would be an example of foreign meddling.

Chile: On September 11, 1973, democratically elected president Allende was overthrown in a coup that was orchestrated and supported by the United States. The new dictator carried out economic policies which caused a severe depression in Chile. So this would be an example both of "foreign meddling" and "turmoil", although this example was not mentioned in the article.

Cuba: This country has been blocked from foreign trade by one single nation, since 1960. That nation is the United States. In the United Nations, every year, the U.N. General Assembly (the nations of the world) perform a non-binding vote to repeal this blockade. (Only the security council nations can make binding votes.) The U.S. typically has one or two countries that vote along with it, and about 180 countries, all the others in the world, voting to remove the blockade. For example:

YEAR:	End the blockade	Retain it
1992	59	2 U.S, & Israel
1993	88	4 U.S., Israel Albania,Paraguay
1994	101	2 U.S. & Israel
1995	117	3 U.S. Israel Uzbekistan
1996	138	3 U.S. Israel Uzbekistan

YEAR	End blockade	Retain it	
1997	143	3	U.S. Israel Uzbekistan
1998	157	2	U.S. & Israel
1999	155	3	US, Israel Marshall Is
2000	167	3	US Israel Marshall Is
2001	167	3	US Israel Marshall IS
2002	167	3	US Israel Marshall Is
2003	173	4	US,Israel, Marshall I Palau
2004	179	4	US,Israel, Marshall I Palau
2005	182	4	US,Israel, Marshall I Palau
2006	183	4	US,Israel, Marshall I Palau
YEAR	**End blockade**	**Retain it**	
2007	184	4	US,Israel, Marshall I Palau
2008	185	3	U.S., Israel, Palau
2009	187	3	U.S., Israel, Palau
2010	186	2	U.S. & Israel
2011	186	2	U.S. & Israel
2012	188	2	U.S. & Israel
2013	188	2	U.S., Israel
2014	188	2	U.S., Israel
2015	191	2	U.S., Israel
2016	191	0	Abstained US & Isra
2017	191	2	U.S., Israel
2018	189	2	U.S., Israel

Also, the United States has committed economic sabotage and tried more than 100 times to murder Cuba's leader, Fidel Castro. By blocking trade, both "economic malaise" and "turmoil", another subject discussed in the article, is thus created. These actions also are a violation of international law.

This would be an example of foreign meddling, although this example was not mentioned in the article.

Venezuela: Venezuela has fallen victim to very serious trade sanctions by the United States. One 2019 study by economists Mark Weisbrot and Jeffrey Sachs calculates approximately 40,000 deaths as a direct result of the sanctions. This would be an example of "foreign meddling" and also of "turmoil" created, although this example was not mentioned in the article. A later study by the United Nations put the deaths at 100,000.

The article described Venezuela as a dictatorship. That is incorrect. The last presidential election in Venezuela had foreign observers present, and they all agreed that it was a fair democratic election. Venezuela is a polarized society and the press is owned by those on the other side of the political spectrum of the President and his administration. In Venezuela, the press is very openly anti- government. If Venezuela was truly a dictatorship, then certainly the media would not be permitted to throw out such regular criticisms against their government.

It is not insignificant to note that the election system in Venezuela was described by former U.S. president Jimmy Carter, as "the best election system IN THE WORLD". What qualifies Jimmy Carter to make such a statement? Jimmy Carter developed an organization which monitors elections around the world, and he received a Nobel Peace Prize for providing this service.

The article also states that Juan Guaido is recognized as the legitimate president of Venezuela by dozens of governments, yet it fails to mention that Juan Guaido was never even a candidate for president of Venezuela. 80% of the people of Venezuela first heard his name when the United States was declaring him to be the real "president" of oil rich Venezuela, and the show of many governments suddenly agreeing is a testimony to the power of the United States over many other nations, although 5/6 of the nations of the world (about 150 out of roughly 180) properly recognize Maduro as the president of Venezuela, because he ran for the position as a candidate, and was chosen by a majority of the voters, in an election that included international election monitors who certified the results, in the country that, according to Nobel Prize winning election monitoring director Jimmy Carter referred to as having the best election system in the world.

Part of the article calls out Cuba, and incorrectly, Venezuela as dictatorship, but it does not mention that according to a very conservative study, it was found that 73% of all of the dictatorships on planet Earth, receive regular military aid from the United States. By supplying military aid to dictatorships, that helps those in power to remain in power, making change much less possible or probable. Most people don't want to live under dictatorships and want to change those forms of government, so, that can be looked at as a form of foreign meddling that causes turmoil, although this example was also not mentioned in the article.

For foreign investors, in respect to an export related national economy, dictatorships are a more reliable form of government that can more easily dictate how the society is going to work, and who it is going to work for.

Furthermore, the dictatorships that the United States support are right wing dictatorships. Right wing policies focus on concentration of wealth in the hands of the few, and this ultimately causes economic malaise – which was mentioned in the article as the underlying cause of the protests.

So as Americans, if we are discussing dictatorships as if they are something less than positive, then should not the discussion immediately revolve around how to change U.S. foreign policy? A good question to ask Foreign Affairs Magazine.

In Chile the people are protesting because of the rise in the cost of living, making everyday life truly a challenge there. I typed in the following in Google search engine: "reasons for the protests in Chile" and this is what came up: 2019 Chilean protests: Rise in public transport fares, rising cost of living; income inequality; privatization; corruption scandals.

In Ecuador essentially the same problem is happening there as well. The cut of fuel subsidies resulted in diesel fuel prices doubling and regular fuel prices increasing 30 percent, angering transportation unions and businesses who started the protest movement. Businesses also panicked, leading to speculation, with a range of everyday costs spiking rapidly shortly after the decision. With the increase in fuel prices, a general increase in all prices ensues due to added transportation costs.

What is causing this rise in fuel prices? Two of the world's largest oil producing countries are being prevented from putting their oil on the world market, causing an artificial shortage, and thus a rise in prices. Those countries are Iran and Venezuela. What force is preventing them from putting their oil on the world market? Sanctions from a foreign nation – known in Latin America as E.U. or Estados Unidos. Here in the U.S. that translates as follows: *The United States.*

The article continues: "Thanks to a boom in commodities prices, driven largely by demand from China, Latin American economies grew by an average of 3.5 percent on a per capita basis between 2003 and 2013, their best performance in at least half a century. These gains were relatively well distributed."

The article then goes on to explain: "The specifics vary country to country, but there are some common causes for the regional downturn. Many Latin American governments were left with unsustainably large budget deficits at the end of the commodities boom and failed to adjust quickly enough to REASSURE INVESTORS" (emphasis added).

In response to that claim, I quote from a paper from economists Mark Weisbrot and David Rosnick of the Center for Economic and Policy Research titled: "Latin American Growth in the 21st Century – the "Commodities Boom" that wasn't.

"Latin America's economic growth rebound in the 2000's does not appear to have resulted from a commodities boom" as is often suggested, as there is no statistically significant relationship between the increase in the terms of trade for Latin American countries and their GDP growth." "Improved terms of trade can help countries avoid current account imbalances, but their direct impact on economic growth has often been overstated." "Other factors, such as macro-economic policy choices, may have been more important."

Regarding macro-economic policy choices mentioned above, note that the 2000 World Development Report entitled "Attacking Poverty", (World Bank 2000, chapter 3) makes a case for redistribution to the poor, noting that poverty is inextricably tied to income inequality, rather than overall economic growth.

Again, the article looks at the period between 2003 and 2013 as the best economic performance in at least half a century. It ties this to a commodity boom, however, during that period, Latin America had left leaning leadership that replaced the previous right leaning leadership, and that, I would argue, is the real reason for the economic growth;

Hugo Chavez – president of Venezuela 1993 – 2013

Lula da Silva – president of Brazil 2003 – 2010

Nestor Kirchner – president of Argentina 2003 – 2007

Cristina Fernandez de Kirchner – Argentina 2007 – 2015

Rafael Correa – president of Ecuador 2007 – 2017

Ivo Morales – president of Bolivia 2006 – 2019

Daniel Ortega – president of Nicaragua 2007 to current

There is no coincidence here. Left leaning leadership is what was responsible for the economic growth, not the "commodities boom" story.

Notice the new Right Wing leadership now in South America:

Sebastian Pinera - Chile– 12/17/17 to present

Mauricio Macri - Argentina – 12/10/15 to present

Lenin Moreno – Ecuador – 5/24/17 to present

Jair Bolsonaro – Brazil – 1/1/19 to present

Jeanine Añez – Bolivia 11/20/19 to present

Let's look at an instructive example from another country which is not in Latin America but which is a very important, large country and therefore a very important example. The country in question is located in North America - the United States.

In Larry Bartel's book "Unequal Democracy", a study of macro-economic performance under Democratic vs Republican presidents is presented, covering the period of 1948 – 2005. The book was published in 2008. The results of this review of 58 years of U.S. modern economic history revealed that:

"the average level of unemployment over the post-war era has been almost 30% higher under Republican presidents than under Democrats, while the average rate of real per capital GNP (Gross National Product) growth has been more than 40% lower (under Republicans). However, despite Republican traditional emphasis on curbing inflation, the average inflation rate has been virtually identical under Republican and Democratic presidents over this period." (Hibbs).

Republicans, or Conservatives claim to be stronger on the economy than Democrats or liberals, but the fact is that the exact opposite is true. Republicans side with those who are already wealthy to begin with while liberals side more with the general public as an integrated whole. Since a national economy has its basis in consumption of goods and services, (about 70% in the U.S.) and it is the general public that would be doing most of such consumption, policies that try not to squeeze the poor, that prevent the rich from holding on to too much of the wealth, will stimulate overall economic performance.

The art of successful governance comes in finding the natural balance point, based on the circumstances, in order to maintain optimum health of an economy. So clearly, it is in no way controversial to note that in respect to issues related to a national economy, the Left have the more critical analysis of this balance. That is what the empirical evidence tells us, in spite of this other analysis from Foreign Policy Magazine.

So why economic malaise? The U.S. and a few other countries control too much economic weight in Latin America through their international organizations and their multi-national corporations, and notice also, for example, the tremendous damage that U.S. economic sanctions can cause.

Causes of Economic Malaise:

1. Put in the "right" leader.

The U.S. puts in leaders who will do what the U.S. wants. Numerous examples will be provided later in this chapter. The U.S. puts in corrupt monsters who know that if they don't do as they are told, that they too will be overthrown. Corrupt leaders are the ones who are looking out for their own interests and the interests of their own circle, and do not care as much for the needs of others. People like Juan Guaido, for example, who would proclaim himself president of Venezuela, when in fact, he never even ran for the office. People down at the C.I.A. know very well that corrupt people are the ones who are the most easily controlled.

2. What does the U.S. want?

The "U.S." wants free access to foreign economies so that our multi-national corporations can operate with impunity in order to maximize their profits, Places that don't have labor laws or environmental laws or much of any local taxes, with minimal or zero taxes to the State will yield greater profits to U.S. corporations.

The "U.S." wants tyrannical leaders that will quell public dissent and control the public in order to make those countries more ideal places for international investors to make greater profit margins. This is achieved by cheating the public and oppressing their resulting dissent.

World Trade Organization (WTO) rules were written by a group of U.S. Corporate attorneys for the benefit of those corporations. "Free Trade" agreements provide for governments to open their doors to international players. This ultimately results in a foreign takeover by giant U.S. corporations of whole economies of smaller developing nations of people who are trying to rise from hundreds of years of oppressive foreign Spanish rule, only to become victims of foreign multi-national corporate rule. For example, how can the corner store in Quito Ecuador compete with a Walmart store? So the successful businesses become foreign owned businesses that take their profits out of those foreign countries instead of investing back into those foreign national economies and communities.

What do we mean by the "U.S."

By the U.S., I am not referring to the American general public, I mean the people who sit in Board of Directorship for U.S. corporations, who corporate lobbyists are lobbying for, and large contributors to political campaigns. (see Giants by Phillips) Opinion polls consistently show that the U.S. general public wants U.S. foreign policy to express fairness and justice. (See "The Foreign Policy Disconnect" by Page and Simmons)

Aside from picking its leaders, by what methodology does the U.S. accomplish gaining control of foreign economies, mainly in the third world?

The answer to that is through the use of three powerful global institutions: The World Bank, The World Trade Organization (WTO) and the International Monetary Fund (IMF).

By what methods does the U.S. overthrow foreign governments?

A very well financed agency of the U.S. government, the CIA is involved in more than national defense, and the same can also be said for the entire Department of Defense.

U.S. foreign embassies typically house CIA operatives. Nations that are poor and weak are considered fair game. Strong Western nations are not targeted. Countries that are high in natural resources are prioritized. Countries that have nationalist independent economic policies that lean to the left of the political spectrum are going to be the sworn enemies of the United States government, because left leaning countries give first priority to the welfare of their own citizens, and more for them means less of their resources for "us" the wealthy people here in the West. Also, success, such as in countries like Nicaragua and Venezuela show the world that there is another way, and this has to be extinguished, ASAP, according to our leaders.

Countries that are run by dictators who follow the prescriptions of the WTO and the IMF are referred to as "fledgling democracies" and are our allies, and the U.S. government tells the press that we are trying to teach them to improve their human rights and increase their democratic structures, but of course that never happens.

Not everybody in the U.S. foreign policy establishment agrees with such policies.

Meticulous examples of this have been provided by many authors. The ones that I have read are; William Blum, Noam Chomsky, Mark Curtis, Dana Frank, Eva Golinger, Amy Goodman, Melvin Goodman, Greg Grandin, Chalmers Johnson, Stephen Kinser, Greg Palast, Michael Parenti, John Perkins, John Pilger, John Stockwell, Nick Turse and Douglas Valentine.

Max Blumenthal is also writing about this subject matter, although I have not read his work, and I am sure that there are others. Phillip Agee wrote about this subject matter many years ago, and I have not read his work. There are many more authors who cover this subject, but who write in more general terms. Chris Hedges might be an example of this, although I have not read all of his works.

Essentially, the U.S. government makes contact with opposition leaders and finances the ones who they believe will follow the prescriptions that will make such countries allies. They have a group they call the National Endowment for Democracy (NED) that does this work

The National Endowment for Democracy (NED) was established in the early 80's under President Reagan in the wake of the negative public revelations about the CIA which surfaced in the Church Committee of the Senate and the Pike Commission in Congress. Many of the functions that were performed by the CIA were moved to this organization with the positive sounding name.

The official description of this agency's purpose was to "support democratic institutions throughout the world through private Non-governmental efforts." However, this agency is actually in reality part of the U.S. government.

Allen Weinstein, who helped to draft the legislation that established the NED stated in 1991: "A lot of what we do today was done covertly 25 years ago by the CIA."

The basic philosophy of the NED is minimal government intervention in the economy and opposition to socialism in any measure or form.

One example of their work: From 1994 – 1996 they awarded 15 grants totaling more than 2.5 million dollars to the American Institute for Free Labor Development, an organization used by the CIA for decades, to subvert progressive labor unions.

This organization goes to third world countries that have social safety nets and economic developmental planning, and funds right wing opposition parties who oppose governments who serve the aspirations of most of its citizens in favor of big business running the show with a few living like kings and the many having to support that and pay for it with their daily work, in poverty. So this is really, in effect, an extension of the U.S. Republican party, that travels around the world to interfere in foreign elections.

NED funds various organizations who in turn can fund other organizations who in turn can fund yet other organizations, and all the funds originate with the U.S. government.

Another tool used by the government is propaganda. The CIA has in the past purchased foreign newspapers and printed false stories that are eventually picked up by U.S. media outlets and the stories are ultimately quoted and referred to by opposition figures in target nations. (see William Blum)

The U.S. government's Drug Enforcement Agency (DEA) is employed to make contacts with military figures in foreign countries and offer special military training. These liaisons offer opportunities to find potential future dictators and or individuals who will be able to take over the military forces of the target nations. This also happens when the U.S. Government agrees to sell U.S. military equipment to foreign countries.

If you want to read a serious account of how our drug enforcement agency has been corrupted by the CIA, I recommend reading the books by Douglas Valentine. Also, it is an interesting fact that after several decades, we haven't been able to make any headway yet on our "war on drugs".

U.S. representatives also engage in bullying behavior during diplomatic forums.

The U.S. Government makes extensive use of spying on electronic communications and telephone conversations through the NSA, and they have spied, for example, on officers of the United Nations, and even on the president of Germany, Angela Merkel.

While I agree that we must have national security and a certain level of spying, which I'm sure that many nations engage in, and I agree with having a Department of Defense, I, along with most Americans (based on opinion polls), feel that there are unassailable ethical issues if such instruments are to be used for purposes other than strictly defense.

Sabotage has also been used against Cuba, Venezuela, Nicaragua, and in other places, along with False Flag operations, as I believe is now happening with Iran. A False Flag operation is where an incident is caused by the U.S. and then blamed on the target. In both Ukraine and Venezuela, for example, snipers shot to kill people on both sides of a demonstration in order that either protestors can be blamed for violence they did not create, causing a violent crackdown on popular demonstrations, or in other cases, to blame a targeted government for committing violence against its own citizens, thereby applying world wide public pressure on the targeted government officials.

Lee Camp wrote an excellent article for Truthdig.com dated 8/22/18 titled "How to Create A U.S.-Backed Government Coup for Fun & Profit!";

Step One: Create a strong U.S.-backed "fifth column". A fifth column is defined as a group of people who undermine the Government of a country in support of the enemy.

Step Two: Undermine the Country's economy.

Step Three: Wait for internal protests and/or create them.

Step Four: Get violent while accusing the government of getting violent.

Step Five: If steps 1 through 4 don't work, kidnap or assassinate.

This article, which I very briefly summarized, is very well done, and I highly recommend Lee Camp's show found on You-Tube called Redacted Tonight. Lee Camp is also quite funny.

So I think that I have covered the methodology – at least on an introductory level.

6. How can this happen if the general public wants justice in our foreign policy?

For one thing, this is the endeavor of wealthy and conservative people who are helped psychologically in their endeavor by a racist ideology, and unlimited greed.

Around the world, a correlation has been found in the field of Psychology with Conservatism and Racism. Conservatives see the world differently than do people on the left.

"People on the right have higher authoritarianism scores than do people on the left" (Pratto)

Felicia Pratto of the University of Connecticut, co-author of "Social Dominance: An Intergroup Theory of Social Hierarchy and Oppression" wrote the following:

"Just as authoritarianism theorists speculated, there really does appear to be a phenomenon we may call generalized ethnocentrism, reflecting itself in the denigration of a wide range of outgroups, including ethnic groups, political groups, sexual orientation groups, and stigmatized religious groups. Second, this generalized tendency to stigmatize and denigrate the generalized "other" contains a consistent theme of dominance and submission. Third, generalized ethnocentrism is positively associated with political conservatism.

THIS ASSOCIATION HAS BEEN FOUND CONSISTENTLY ACROSS A WIDE VARIET OF CULTURES AND HAS BEEN FOUND SO CONSISTENT THAT SOME THEORISTS HAVE EVEN CONSIDERED ETHNOCENTRISM AS A DEFINITIONAL COMPONENT OF CONSERVATISM." (emphasis added)

So, a conservative leader is a leader with less empathy and less compassion. Furthermore, people involved with State security, Policing, and the Armed Forces, are also found to be highly conservative.

Let's look at some more examples of direct U.S. interference in Latin America.

Brazil, 1964

In 1964, progressive president Joao Goulart was overthrown by elements of the Brazilian military who were aided by the U.S. government.

The Goulart government had passed a law limiting the amount of profits that multinationals could transmit out of the country. Goulart had plans for popular social reforms and he pointed out that General MacArthur had carried out a far more radical distribution of land in Japan after the second world war than what he wanted to do in

But he was overthrown anyway.

After the coup, the coup government proceeded to practice widespread torture and murder, but they reversed Goulart's reforms and thus enjoyed the support of the U.S. government. The U.S. government did not then and does not now truly care about the welfare of people around the world. They care if U.S. businesses can increase their wealth, and it does not matter how that wealth gets increased.

To give you a flavor of the U.S. ally government, the following is a quote from the chief of staff of the Brazilian army at the time, General Breno Borges Forte in 1973 at the tenth conference of American Armies:

"The enemy is undefined... it adapts to any environment and uses every means, both licit and illicit to achieve its aims. It disguises itself as a priest, a student or a campesino, as a defender of democracy or an advanced intellectual, as a pious soul or as an extremist protester."

So, perhaps supporting evil may not be such a good idea.

Guatemala 1963

In 1963 General Ydigoras was overthrown in a military coup. Reporter Georgie Anne Geyer later reported the following: "Top sources within the Kennedy administration have revealed that the U.S. instigated and supported the coup.

Ydigoras had allowed Juan Jose Arevalo, who had earlier led a reform government, to return to Guatemala, and Arevlo had a strong following in Guatemala. Ydigoras was planning to step down in 1964. Kennedy believed that a free election would result in Arevalo being elected, and the U.S. would not allow the will of the people of Guatemala to prevail in the next Guatemalan election. Note also that Arevalo had denounced Castro as a menace to the Western Hemisphere – a highly pro American position. But he was overthrown anyway.

Jamaica in the 1970's

Michael Manley, a graduate from the London School of Economics, was elected President of Jamaica. He called himself a Democratic Socialist. His policies matched what could be found at the time in many countries of Western Europe. His government imposed a levy against transnational American owned mining companies.

Two investigative reporters, in a 1977 article in Penthouse magazine reported that several senior American intelligence sources were discussing a destabilization grogram which entailed sending arms shipments and communication devices to opposition groups in Jamaica.

Not long thereafter, a shipment of 50 sub machine guns was intercepted by the government security forces of Jamaica. The C.I.A. also sent in a traveling army of Cuban exiles. Violence erupted which among other things, killed the tourist business.

The C.I.A. was operating a labor organization called the American Institute for Free Labor Development, and graduates of this organization organized a number of strikes in Jamaica.

Shipments of flour and rice that were received on the island were later found to have been poisoned, killing 17 people, reminiscent of the contaminated sugar that had been sent to Cuba by U.S. government channels.

There were 3 unsuccessful assassination attempts on Manley's life and he was able to finish his term as president but failed to win re-election.

I believe that I made a point with these three examples plus the seven other examples listed earlier.

The Foreign Affairs article ends by providing advice to all of Latin America as follows: "leaders across the region should identify the top two or three priorities for their countries – for example, malnutrition in the Northern Triangle countries of Central America, security in Mexico or Brazil, infrastructure in Colombia, modernization of schools everywhere – and convene broad coalitions to address them.) (To effectively address these problems, governments, businesses, and civil society must collaborate. People will need to put their mobile phones aside for a moment and stop expecting governments to solve all of their problems."

So that's what the article has to offer, ignoring the blood thirsty neighbor to the north, directed by the Council on Foreign Relations. The article doesn't mention the relevant factors and does not reach the correct conclusions.

So let's make a comparison in tone. This article ends with: "People will need to put their mobile phones aside for a moment and stop expecting governments to solve all of their problems." Let's contrast that statement with the first sentence in the introduction of the book "Global Capitalism and the Crisis of Humanity" by professor William I. Robinson:

"Our world is burning. We face a global crisis that is unprecedented in terms of its magnitude, its global reach, the extent of ecological degradation and social deterioration, and the scale of the means of violence."

Here's a quote from author Michael Parenti, a P.H.D Yale graduate in Political Science:

"Throughout history, there has been only one thing that ruling interests have ever wanted – and that is everything: all the choice lands, forests, game, herds, harvests, mineral deposits, and precious metals of the earth; all the wealth, riches, and profitable returns; all the productive facilities, gainful inventiveness, and technologies; all the control positions of the state and other major institutions; all public supports and subsidies, privileges and immunities; all the protections of law with none of its constraints; all the services, comforts, luxuries, and advantages of civil society with none of the taxes and costs. Every ruling class has wanted only this: all the rewards and none of the burdens. The operational code is: we have a lot, we can get more; we want it all."

If the wider general public in the developed countries would become better acquainted with these facts, things would change for the better

What can Latin American nations do in order to experience economic growth?

For starters, Hugo Chavez, who presided over tremendous economic growth in Venezuela, strove for more regional integration, a regional trade organization regional banking, and a clearer and more public understanding of the nemesis that they all face from the north. Chavez infuriated the American establishment by pointing out that the United States represents a grave threat to the Sovereignty of all of Latin America. Chavez died a mysterious death when he contracted both colon cancer and had heart attacks at a young age of only 58.

Lula da Silva, who presided over tremendous economic growth in Brazil put all types of public assistance together into one integrated program which helped the Federal government to collect more tax revenues, also making it more difficult for so much of the economy to operate informally, as recipients had to register, and thus become subject to paying taxes. Lula da Silva was jailed on trumped up charges, preventing him from running for a third term.

Latin America's purpose in global Capitalism, is to provide cheap labor and low cost raw materials so that wealthy people in the North can rake off most of the value. Recognizing that they are operating as the bottom of the "food chain" Latin America has to re-write its own rules and extricate itself from the claims of global capitalism. This is a very dangerous scenario, so it will possibly take a very long time to do so with a long series of steps. It has no chance of doing so without a completely united front among all of these nations. As individual nations, they can be picked off one by one, but if they find a way to all hang together, then it's a different ballgame. If Global Capitalism is going to treat Latin America solely as a supply of cheap labor, then Latin America needs to shut out global capital and protect their own industries from foreign competition. This is how all the developed nations of the world have developed historically, especially the United States which used to lead the world with a 40% trade tariff. The greatest threat would come from those who are wealthy and who are looking after principally their own interests.

The nations of South America have to agree that if the United States is to be trusted, then it needs to prove itself as trustworthy. Latin America needs to demand that the United States government educate its people on how it has operated and on how it operates in respect to international trade in the third world

Latin America needs to demand that the U.S. government inform its own people about all the coups and bloodshed that it is has been responsible for.

Latin America needs to demand that the U.S. do what it needs to do in order to prevent global warming from destroying all life on earth.

Latin America needs to demand that laws are passed in the United States that provide a media court where people can sue media companies for faulty reporting of the facts, resulting in injunctions, forcing certain news coverages, or, in the case of Fox News, a loss of their license to broadcast over the public airwaves.

Latin America needs to demand that the United States pass some radical campaign finance reform, and that those who wish to run for public office be able to pass some tests that demonstrate some basic knowledge in sociology, and proof of some empathy – some feelings for other people.

Without this, the United States is destined to be nothing more than just a rogue state that cannot be trusted to be anything less than a major player in organized crime.

Latin America must demand that the United States remove all of their 800 or so military bases that they have situated outside their borders. Without that, the U.S. is a threat to peace everywhere.

Latin America must demand that the corporate charter in the United States be changed to include several meaningful caveats to just the maximization of profit, including protecting the community in terms of jobs and environment. Failing that, doing business with U.S. corporations would be doing business with voracious entities that will be engaged in dangerous sociopathic behavior.

These steps would be needed in order to establish diplomatic relations on new terms – on better footing, and not only to make economic growth more possible for Latin America, but also for the United States, which has very serious problems as a nation, stemming from the inequality and the use of so much of its government funds for the military instead of for social and economic supports for its people.

Although I must say that I don't believe that the ruling classes in Latin American countries, aided by the United States, will allow this to happen, and therefore these countries will remain in poverty and turmoil.

When a Latin American country has a left leaning government, they need to put rich and powerful citizens, and military leaders alike, under constant surveillance, as this is where the Coups come from.

Military cooperation with the U.S. must be prohibited, as this is a well known cause of coups. Even cooperation against drug running is another way that governments eventually get overthrown. Permitting your military to train in the U.S. is one more thing to prohibit in order to prevent coups. The American Embassy must be under constant surveillance, and the only way to deal with the U.S. embassy staff, who are largely CIA, is through entrapment programs, similar to what the FBI does, using people who are pretending to be someone else in order to uncover the plots.

American embassies must be minimized in number and by number of staff. But most importantly, the general public must be educated regarding the long history of U.S. subversion of foreign states. Public schools need to include this in their curriculum, before it's too late.

The United States should change the way they operate and look to the best interests of all peoples. Failing that, they should be quarantined to prevent causing any more damage to people who are just struggling to meet the challenges of every-day life.

Aside from the above discussion, a publication such as Foreign Affairs should review the fact that not only the trade regiment of United States, but also of the European Union and Japan are all very much in favor of the current WTO. A publication such as this should look at this status quo and how can the enormous power of the United States be used in order to change it so that a developed nation will not be severely penalized by the other developed nations simply because they are following basic moral principles.

It can be instructive to look at power relations and how these forces add up, but without then applying a moral tone to the discussion, then we are nothing more than a band of pirates, which is what we are now.

Let's now look at an article by Thomas Graham called
"Let Russia be Russia".

Mr. Graham starts out repeating everything that has been
stated in the main stream news, therefore allowing him
to be accepted as an Establishment writer, although he
contradicts himself a number of times. I guess that in
order to be an Establishment writer on Russia you would
have to be self- contradictory because the subject matter
as expressed in main stream outlets is so filled with lies.

Thomas Graham is a Distinguished Fellow at the Council
on Foreign Relations and served as a Senior Director for
Russia on the National Security Council staff during the
George W. Bush administration.

It's hard to know how to begin this... Mr. Graham noted:
"It was misguided to ground U.S. policy in the
assumption that Russia would join the community of
liberal Democratic nations."

How could they? Economist Jeffrey Sachs was invited by
the Russian government to help them with the transition
to capitalism. Here is his account of what happened, as
he wrote on page 137 of his book "The End of Poverty".

"Russia would need considerable international help to pull
all of this off successfully, including the now-familiar
components of financial reserves for stabilization of the
Russian currency, the ruble, and cancellation of part of the
Soviet-era debt."

"I called repeatedly for a $15 billion per year aid program
to enable Russia to stabilize the currency, introduce a

social safety net for pensioners and other vulnerable groups, and to help restructure industry. I thought that $15 billion per year was not too much to ask, since it was a tiny fraction of 1 percent of the income of the rich world, and a tiny fraction of the annual spending for armaments to fight the cold war." "This view was not accepted in Washington."

"I advocated three immediate actions by the West to support Russia's transformation: A stabilization fund for the ruble, as there had been for Poland. An immediate suspension of debt payments, followed by deep cancellation of Russia's debts. A new aid program for transformation, focusing on the most vulnerable social sectors of the Russian economy."

Sachs did not receive the help he had requested.

Page 140: "I had supposed in 1991 and 1992 that the United States would be rooting for Russia's success as it had been rooting for Poland's. With hindsight, I doubt that this was ever the case."

Dick Cheney and Paul Wolfowitz, the main people who gave us the war in Iraq, were in the administration back in the early 90's. "Given the zero-sum thinking that Cheney and Wolfowitz have propounded, it now seems plausible to me that bolstering Russia's quick recovery was viewed as inimical to U.S. interests by the White House of George H. W. Bush and the defense establishment."

By 1995 and 1996 Russian privatization of industries got out of hand. Sachs was seeing how corrupt people were ending up with all the wealth, which would move Russia into an oligarchy. He saw these schemes forming.

"I tried to warn the U.S. government, the IMF, the Organization for Economic Cooperation and Development, and other G7 governments. I told them that I knew the players in this affair, and that the process was utterly disreputable." "The West let this happen without a murmur."

In other words, the West just sat by and let Russia become an oligarchy.

Here is another account by another economist, Nobel prize winner Joseph Stiglitz, former chief economist of the World Bank and former chairman of the U.S. President's council of economic advisors. He said this in his book Globalization and its Discontents Revisited: Page 360:

"the way the IMF and the U.S. Treasury managed the transition in Russia and elsewhere helped create the oligarchs." "In particular, I worried that the way the IMF, the World Bank, and the U.S. Treasury pushed privatization and the transition more generally in Russia would undermine democratic development there, and that is indeed what happened."

Here is another account by another economist, Michael Hudson, President of the Institute for the Study of Long Term Economic Trends: "The IMF and World Bank wiped out Russian savers with a hyper- inflation by getting rid of all the capital controls and letting the rouble float. So it was just one bad advice after another and now the Russians realize they've been taken. And they're trying to figure out how on earth do we get out of this mess following the West's advice.

They thought, and the Baltics thought, that they were being told how to develop in the way that the West did. Neo-liberalism is the exact opposite of how Britain and the United States, Germany, Japan, and now China, got rich- by progressive taxation, and having public infrastructure provided at much lower cost than privatized infrastructure and a resource fund tax, basically a land tax which is how

Europe and America – states and localities – have been financed all throughout their history."

In a number of places in this article, it says that Russia has interfered in U.S. elections and on page 34 it says: "continues to interfere in elections." There is no proof to back up this statement. It has been reported in main stream media that the Russian government hacked a Democratic National Committee (DNC) computer and gave Hillary Clinton's e-mails to Wikileaks to publish them in order to hurt their campaign. (The thinking, unstated, is that this would help Trump because we can't find out what Hillary really thinks because then we wouldn't vote for her.)

This was debunked. The Magazine "The Nation", in an article dated 8/9/17 titled "A New Report Raises Big Questions About Last Year's DNC Hack", reported on a study of this "hack" by several veteran intelligence professionals and the conclusion was that the data left the DNC computer at a transfer rate of 22.7 megabytes per second. The fastest internet provider at that time would only be able to provide a transfer rate of 15.6 megabytes per second, but even slower than that for a trans-oceanic data transfer. Therefore, the data was copied by a person standing next to the computer and inserting a type of thumb drive or data storage device. So this was not an internet hack, it was a leak by an insider.

Some of the people who were involved in this study were William Binney, formerly the NSA's technical director for world geopolitical and military analysis, and designer of many programs for the NSA, Kirk Wiebe, a former senior analyst at the NSA's Sigint Automation Research Center, Edward Loomis, former technical director in the NSA's office of Signal Processing; and Ray McGovern, former chief of the CIA's Soviet Foreign Policy branch.

So this is the hack that never happened. Now let's discuss the internet company that was indicted.

The FBI generated an indictment against 13 Russian citizens who were working for a Russian marketing company called Internet Research Agency. They would put out ads on hot subjects to try to create a viewership in order ultimately to make money on advertising. Robert Muller was in charge of this investigation which resulted in this indictment. Remember that Robert Muller was one of the people who appeared in front of Congress to explain that Iraq had weapons of mass destruction and that there was no time, that we had to attack. So Mr. Muller may be many things, but it cannot be considered controversial to note that it would be more than fair to say that Mr. Muller a political hack.

The Vice President of Advertising for Facebook, Rob Goldman noted: "The majority of the Russian ad spending happened AFTER the election. We shared that fact, but very few outlets have covered it because it doesn't align with the main media narrative of Trump and the election." Also, Rob Goldman said: "I have seen all of the Russian ads and I can say very definitively that swaying the election was NOT the main goal."

How on earth would Russia come to believe that they would be able to influence a U.S. presidential election? And get away with it? That is the most expensive election on the planet. And with 13 people? THINK!! The article also points out that Russia's economy measures only a fraction of ours. How are they going to come up with the billions needed and who would believe that they would think that they could get away with it without being sanctioned? This is just a story that falls apart immediately on inspection.

So now we know that Russia DOES NOT try to influence our elections.

The article starts out on page 134 stating "Since the end of the cold war, every U.S. president has come into office promising to build better relations with Russia – and each one has watched that vision evaporate." Clinton, Bush and Obama are mentioned, and it continues with "Each left office with relations in worse shape than he found them, and with Russia growing ever more distant." But then on page 137 & 138 "The Clinton Administration for the most part got its way, intervening in the Balkans and expanding NATO." Then on page 144 it notes that "Bush withdrew from the Anti-Ballistic treaty, expanded NATO further, and welcomed the so-called Color Revolutions in Georgia and Ukraine, with their anti—Russian overtones." Also on page 138, when Obama was president: "Washington also paid little heed to Russia's objections when the United States and its allies exceeded the terms of the U.N. Security mandate to protect an endangered population into an operation to overthrow the country's strongman, Muammar Qaddafi."

Regarding that above statement "mandate to protect an endangered population", to be clear, that endangered population in question was in fact Al Queda, and their strong presence in Benghazi. This point is delved into in more detail later on.

So the author first explains how three U.S. presidents had expressed "a desire to strengthen their ties with Russia, but only to watch that vision evaporate", "with Russia growing ever more distant", and then, throughout the article, the descriptions of actions taken by the U.S. very clearly demonstrates exactly why Russia would be cool to the U.S. It seems as though the author can't simply spell it out – as he would lose the respect of his readers because of a strong, emotional anti-Russian sentiment that the mass media has worked so hard to create over such a long period of time. Perhaps he has to carefully plant this information so that it may fall into the readers subconscious at some "aha" moment sometime in the future.

On page 139 it says "Putin has inserted Russia as a major player in many geopolitical conflicts, most notably in Syria", yet, on page 138 it says: "Russia's military intervention in Syria saved Assad from imminent defeat at the hands of **U.S. backed rebels.**" And then on page 141 it says: "Putin intervened in Syria both to protect a long-standing client and to prevent the victory of **radical Islamist forces** with ties to extremists inside Russia." (my emphasis added) With this emphasis that I added, this author now joins the party, the large number of analysts who state that the U.S. was backing radical Islamist forces in Syria to overthrow Assad. Among these forces, Al Queda and Al Nusra.

To repeat, on page 139 it says "Putin has inserted Russia as a major player in many geo political conflicts" and then on page 141 an example is given: "Russia has teamed up with Iran and Turkey to seek a final political resolution of the crisis in Syria. To reduce the risk of a direct conflict between Iran and Israel, Russia has strengthened its diplomatic ties to Israel. It has rebuilt relations with Egypt and worked with Saudi Arabia to manage oil Prices." So these examples look clearly like constructive behavior, but in spite of that, he continues with: "Moscow's more assertive foreign policy today is a reflection not of the country's growing strength – in absolute terms, its power hasn't increased much – but of the perception that the U.S. disarray has magnified Russia's relative power."

So this statement insinuates that Russia's foreign policy is just a reaction to bedevil the United States. What nonsense. And his earlier statements show Russia being involved in constructive actions, but of course, in their interest. I find myself disappointed reading this. I think that Russia does what it feels that it needs to do, and that the thought is how to help Russia, and that the U.S. is not in that equation.

On page 138 the article notes that ("Russia's seizure of Crimea") ("shocked the Obama administration").

So let's clear that up. Russia did not seize Crimea. The local government representatives in Crimea put out a referendum for the people to vote on, that Crimea would become part of Russia. The background events are easy to follow. Ukraine had a violent Coup, and the new administration were very anti-Russian and they even dropped the Russian language as an official language in Ukraine. The people in Crimea – who are Russian speaking people - voted to join Russia and this vote was certified by international observers. The BBC news on 3/16/14 reported that approximately 93% supported the referendum to join Russia. Three months later, Gallup, an American based polling company re-confirmed the preference to join Russia. Forbes magazine reported "The Crimeans are happy right where they are." Eight months later, a German polling company confirmed the local preferences of the people of Crimea to become a part of Russia.

Referendums had been held in former Yugoslavia regarding the separation of the state into statelets, and the West made no protests and accepted it. So there is a precedent.

On page 139 it says "Personal wealth and social position are ultimately dependent on the good graces of those in power." Which suggests to me that Putin is corrupt, yet, on page 138 it says "Russia's economy rapidly recovered after Putin took office and restored order by clamping down on the Oligarchs and regional Barons.", which gives exactly the opposite information. On this subject, I had read in a blog that Putin had invited 17 Oligarchs to the Kremlin where he told them that they were free to keep their wealth under two conditions, that they pay their taxes, and that they stay far removed from politics.

On page 140 it says "(Russia has sought to undermine Washington's standings) ("and has tried to tarnish the United States' image as a paragon of Democratic virtue by interfering in its elections and exacerbating domestic discord.") but on page 146 it says "The media and the political class have exaggerated the threat, blaming Russia for domestic discord."

People involved in national security have complained that R.T. broadcasts into the U.S. are designed to cause domestic discord. I can say from my own experience with R.T. that this is patently false. R.T. has shows with American progressives who look at social problems and ways to solve them. Their shows are more designed for concerned citizens and are not simply entertainment. The people who say such things about R.T. are volunteering opinions based on a combination of conjecture combined with an expectation of finding something terribly wrong.

This article made a number of good points, that Washington & Moscow should develop a new arms control regime, that cooperating with Russia is essential to grappling with critical global challenges such as climate change, nuclear proliferation and terrorism, that the U.S. and other democracies should foster greater awareness of media manipulation.

Clearly, if we stop demonizing Russia, this would result in an existential threat to many employees at the

Pentagon, to the bottom line of the weapons manufacturers and to the long term career objectives of many of the people in the Defense Department and related intelligence organizations.

I for one have my own complaints against Russia. Why do they love baritone singers so much? I certainly don't. Also, they wear funny looking hats in the winter time. Here's one – could it be possible - would we be mad at them for promoting the BRICS trading group which bypasses use of the dollar?....

Chapter 4

The Age of Great Power Competition – page 118 of the Jan/Feb 2020 edition - Foreign Affairs

This article was written by Elbridge Colby, former U.S. Deputy Assistant Secretary of Defense, and A. Wess Mitchell, former U.S. Assistant Secretary of State for European Eurasian Affairs.

"The United States is gearing up for a new era – one marked not by unchallenged U.S. dominance but by a rising China and a vindictive Russia seeking to undermine U.S. leadership and re-fashion global politics in their favor."

This statement expresses the idea that the U.S. plays a leadership role in the world. Let's say that is accurate. Look at where the world is going then, under U.S. leadership:

When the U.S. and Europe adopted Keynesian economic policies, strong economic growth was experienced on a worldwide basis. Since about 1980, the U.S. has switched their economic policies to neoliberalism, which puts corporate activity as the centerpiece of economics, and weakens governments ability to govern and to choose their own economic policies. (See the earlier discussion on the WTO). Globalization has been fostered.

Compared with 1950 – 1980 when Keynesian policies were used, the entire world has seen about a 50% cut in the rate of economic growth, combined with an extreme increase in inequality, causing economic strangulation for literally billions of people. Note that both the WTO and the IMF have been strongly promoted and supported by the United States.

The following is a quote from the book "The Globalization of Poverty" by economist Michel Chussodovsky;

"Humanity is undergoing, in the post-Cold War era, an economic and social crisis of unprecedented scale leading to the rapid impoverishment of large sectors of the world population. National economies are collapsing and unemployment is rampant. Local level famines have erupted in Sub Sahara Africa, South Asia and parts of Latin America. This "globalization of Poverty" – which has largely reversed the achievements of post war decolonization – was initiated in the Third World coinciding with the Debt Crisis of the early 1980's and the imposition of the IMF's deadly economic reforms."

The following is a quote from the book "Global Capitalism and the Crisis of Humanity" by Professor William I. Robinson;

"It is structural violence when 85 percent of the world's wealth is monopolized by just 10 percent of the world's people while the bottom half of adults worldwide owns barely 1 percent of the total (actually, the top 2 percent within the top 10 percent own half the planet's wealth)".

So under U.S. leadership, the world has changed quite dramatically over the last 40 years, in a way that begs the question, is U.S. leadership in the world a positive or is it a negative? Notice how these two gentlemen of such high standing in our society, are discussing who will be the hegemonic power without even addressing the actual state of affairs of the world?

The article "The Age of Great Power Competition" continues:

"For years, American policy makers and analysts have argued about what China's rise and Russia's resurgence mean for U.S. interests." Also *"China – seeking hegemony in the Indo-Pacific region first and global preeminence thereafter-"*

Basically, yes, there is a competition and the only way to win or not to lose too much is by treating other peoples with appropriate fairness, and with earnest concerns for issues of social justice. That's the answer. That which results in loyalty and positive relations in personal affairs, is not all different in the international arena.

The U.S. has always in too many cases relied on having good relations with dictators that we can bully into gaining the best deals of cheap labor and cheap natural resources, with little or no concern for the welfare or the fate of the rank and file citizens of so many foreign nations.

With the rise of China and Russia as "competitors", that cold indifference has to change. It is too easy for even China & Russia to have more to offer foreign nations than the United States.

Currently, the U.S. government provides military support to 73% of the world's dictatorships – dictatorships as defined by Freedom House, and Military Assistance as shown in the Congressional Budget Foreign Assistance Summary Tables, the DOD Security Cooperation Agency, the Foreign Military Training report, and information from the Stockholm International Peace Research Institute.

While providing military support to dictators around the world creates a strong opportunity for investments by companies from the U.S., it conversely creates a very weak structure in a world where there is competition for leadership.

"As China became pivotal to global commerce, it did not so much change its discriminatory economic practices – forced technology transfers, mandatory joint ventures, and outright intellectual property theft – as cement them".

While the authors may demonize these practices, they are nonetheless examples of how virtually all of the developed nations of the world have been able to develop. Ha-Joon-Chang, an economist and professor at Cambridge University notes the following:

"The history of economic development is filled with episodes of industrialization through protective tariffs, import bans, state-owned enterprises, government subsidies over foreign investment and ownership, as well as foreign exchange, and the careful, often prolonged nurturing of infant industries." Also, patenting was only started quite recently in the history of capitalism. Reverse engineering & copying was always the norm throughout history, among what are today referred to as the developed nations. Further reading of Ha-Joon-Chang will explain this history in greater detail.

The article continues;

"Russia, meanwhile, rebuilt its military, invaded Georgia, annexed Crimea, initiated a festering insurgency in Eastern Ukraine, " I would argue that in order to understand any events, it is indispensable to see the context in which such events happen.

James Baker, Ronald Reagan's Secretary of State, promised Gorbachev that NATO would not expand "one inch eastward" after the unification of Germany. Since that promise was made, NATO has added 13 countries that are located near Russia. It turns out that NATO is in fact a military organization that was created for the expressed purpose of being able to defend Europe from Russia. So the authors need to put it into context and notice that a hostile military organization Is moving ever closer to Russia, which causes Russia to feel threatened. It might be helpful to use an example. When Cuba allowed Russia to set up some nuclear missile sites 90 miles from Florida, the United States felt very threatened and demanded that they be removed. That's why Russian Defense minister Sergy Shoigu noted that if Ukraine and/or Georgia were to join NATO, that this would mean the "militarization of the European continent" against Russia.

In an article by analyst Stephen Lendman titled: "Ukraine and Georgia joining NATO crosses an unacceptable red line for Russia", he noted: "During Vladimir Putin's tenure as Russian President, relations with Washington deteriorated markedly, notably after the US – orchestrated coup in Ukraine."

The article from Foreign Affairs continues, stating that Russia *"began a systematic campaign to resurrect its military, economic and diplomatic influence in Africa, Latin America, and the Middle East. And yet most people in Washington long refused to acknowledge the new reality. Instead, American leaders continued to herald an "era of engagement" with Moscow."*

I would respond to that by asking the readers to turn to a different article on page 71 where it says: "States have little or no ability to become economically self-reliant." That means that trade is to be expected among nations – including Russia. To establish foreign trade, diplomatic influence must be established. So what the authors feel threatened by is nothing more than the normal and predictable workings of a state – any state for that matter.

As for the military buildup of Russia, their military spending is estimated to be about 69 billion dollars per year. By comparison, the U.S. military spends more than 700 billion dollars per year – more than ten times what Russia spends.

"In the hopes of recruiting Russia as a partner in upholding an <u>international status quo that Russian President Vladimir Putin manifestly disdained,</u> Washington had courted and unwittingly emboldened the Kremlin on its path of territorial revision." My emphasis added.

What would Putin have against the "international status quo"? For one thing, as a hegemon, the U.S. is able to impose terrible sanctions on foreign nations, and the U.S. has a long history of doing so. If there were valid reasons concerning matters of justice, that's one thing, but a few historical examples say a lot:

A country that had nothing against the U.S., Iraq, was subjected to about thirteen years of sanctions that a U.N. agency said were responsible for the deaths of more than 500,000 children under the age of five, and it was also estimated that approximately another 500,000 people of all the other age groups also died as a direct result of those sanctions. And this was prior to the invasion under George W. Bush. An invasion to protect against weapons of mass destruction – which did not exist.

Another country that has nothing against us, Venezuela, who own their own oil, is another victim of U.S. sanctions. One 2019 study calculates that approximately 40,000 people have died so far as a direct result of the U.S. sanctions.

Cuba has been under U.S. sanctions for over 40 years now, and the entire membership of the U.N. have voted unanimously every year for the past 30 plus years that the U.S. should remove those sanctions. Only one or two countries vote with the U.S., Israel and the Marshall Islands.

So maybe that's why Putin disdains the international status quo. Just a guess.

I find it shocking how these authors failure to see the other side of the coin is so complete, total and monumental. They expect nothing less than total capitulation from other nations. This is a military point of view, not a perspective born of goodwill, respect for the sovereignty of all nations, the needs of others and the desire to live in peace with others in a world of mutual prosperity. Also, in respect to the military aspect of this kind of thinking. Personally, I would characterize this as coming from very low ranking military.

The authors express their alarm at the *"slow-motion takeover attempt in the South China sea", and complain that the U.S. is "unnerving front line NATO allies in eastern Europe. The cost for the United States was steep with allies in east Asia and Europe beginning to doubt that Washington was willing to stand up for itself, let alone for them"*.

So what does that mean? That Washington owns the world including the South China Sea and Eastern Europe? What, that we should have attacked Russia and China militarily? The authors don't say.

How can the U.S. complain about such behavior on the other side of the planet, and at the same time hold on to the best natural port in eastern Cuba, Guantanamo Bay? How can the U.S. justify their presence there while the Cuban government has for many years asked us to leave?

How can these authors then go on to discuss "our problems" in Eastern Europe and in the South China Sea? I thought that the borders of the United States end at the Pacific in the west and the Atlantic in the east, and the Caribbean in the south.

On page 118: *"the United States is gearing up for a new era-one marked not by unchallenged U.S. dominance but by a rising China and* **a vindictive Russia**. *(emphasis added) On the top of page 122 "an opportunistically* **vengeful Russia**. (emphasis added). What do the authors mean? Vengeful for what?

To help explain this, the following is a re print from the book "Unravelling the Puzzle of the Los Angeles Times" by this author, Daniel Silver:

Putin Touts a new nuclear threat   3-2-18 Front Page Los Angeles Times article:

In his annual address to the Federal Assembly in Moscow," Russian president Vladimir Putin boasted Thursday that Russia has developed a new generation of nuclear weapons capable of bypassing any missile defense system".

"Putin's rhetoric, replete with warnings that the Kremlin would respond accordingly to any nuclear attack on Russia or its allies, marked some of the most aggressive language he has deployed in the 13 months that President Trump has been in office."

Thomas Karako, the director of the Missile Defense Project at the Washington based Center for Strategic and International Studies, said") ("This is an example of Russia being provocative, " Karako said. "We have to take that seriously."

OK, I got that. But what about the other half of the story? Isn't there a history behind this which shows how we got to this point? I'm glad you asked.

Let's take a look at an article dated 2/2/18, just one month prior to Putin's speech. The article is from BBC News, titled: "Nuclear Posture Review: US wants smaller nukes to counter Russia."

"The US military has proposed diversifying its nuclear arsenal and developing new, smaller atomic bombs, largely to counter Russia." "The US military is concerned Moscow sees US nuclear weapons as too big to be used – meaning they are no longer an effective deterrent. Developing smaller nukes would challenge that assumption, it argues." The article goes on to discuss how the US military is considering something small such as the bomb that was dropped on Nagasaki during World War II which killed more than 70,000 people."

Am I crazy, or would that be considered provocative? Well, maybe not.

Ok, let's go back 5 weeks prior to this and look at an article by the Los Angeles Times dated 12/26/17: "U.S. decision to provide anti-tank missiles to Ukraine angers Russian leaders" "The Trump administration said earlier in the week that it also would permit sales of some small arms to Ukraine from U.S. manufacturers."

Am I crazy, or would that be considered provocative? Well, maybe not. OK, let's go back a year and 9 months ago to June of 2016. Let's look at an article by the Guardian dated 6/6/16

"Nato countries begin largest war game in eastern Europe since cold war" "Ten-day exercise, Anaconda-2016 will involve 31,000 troops and thousands of vehicles from 24 countries" "It comes within weeks of the US switching on a powerful ballistic missile shield at Deveselu in Romania, as part of a "defense umbrella" that Washington says will stretch from Greenland to the Azores."

Am I crazy, or would that be considered provocative? Well, maybe not. Back in the 60's the Soviet Union had established some missile bases in Cuba, and as we all know, the U.S. didn't find that in any way problematic, did they? Well, they did call it "The Cuban Missile Crisis", so perhaps the U.S. did take issue with it.

OK, let's go back in time and look at the administration of George W. Bush. Did he abandon the 1972 Anti-Ballistic Missile Treaty in 2002 ? Yes he did.

Am I crazy, or would that be considered provocative? Well, maybe not. OK, let's go back to the period when the Soviet Union broke up and switched to Capitalism. The Russian government asked the West for help with the process, and here's what they got:

From "The End of Poverty" by Jeffrey Sachs. Page 137

Jeffrey Sachs was invited by the Russian government to help them with the transition to capitalism. Here is his account of what happened:

"Russia would need considerable international help to pull all of this off successfully, including the now-familiar components of financial reserves for stabilization of the Russian currency, the ruble, and cancellation of part of the Soviet-era debt."

"I called repeatedly for a $15 billion per year aid program to enable Russia to stabilize the currency, introduce a social safety net for pensioners and other vulnerable groups, and to help restructure industry. I thought that $15 billion per year was not too much to ask, since it was a tiny fraction of 1 percent of the income of the rich world,

111

and a tiny fraction of the annual spending for armaments to fight the cold war." "This view was not accepted in Washington."

"I advocated three immediate actions by the West to support Russia's transformation: A stabilization fund for the ruble, as there had been for Poland. An immediate suspension of debt payments, followed by deep cancellation of Russia's debts. A new aid program for transformation, focusing on the most vulnerable social sectors of the Russian economy."

Sachs did not receive the help he had requested.

Page 140: "I had supposed in 1991 and 1992 that the United States would be rooting for Russia's success as it had been rooting for Poland's. With hindsight, I doubt that this was ever the case."

Dick Cheney and Paul Wolfowitz, the main people who gave us the war in Iraq, were in the administration back in the early 90's. "Given the zero-sum thinking that Cheney and Wolfowitz have propounded, it now seems plausible to me that bolstering Russia's quick recovery was viewed as inimical to U.S. interests by the White House of George H. W. Bush and the defense establishment."

By 1995 and 1996 Russian privatization of industries got out of hand. Sachs was seeing how corrupt people were ending up with all the wealth, which would move Russia into an oligarchy. He saw these schemes forming.

"I tried to warn the U.S. government, the IMF, the Organization for Economic Cooperation and Development, and other G7 governments. I told them that I knew the players in this affair, and that the process was utterly disreputable." "The West let this happen without a murmur."

In other words, the West just sat by and let Russia become an oligarchy.

Here is another account by another economist, Nobel prize winner Joseph Stiglitz, former chief economist of the World Bank and former chairman of the U.S. President's council of economic advisors. He said this in his book Globalization and its Discontents Revisited: Page 360:

"the way the IMF and the U.S. Treasury managed the transition in Russia and elsewhere helped create the oligarchs." "In particular, I worried that the way the IMF, the World Bank, and the U.S. Treasury pushed privatization and the transition more generally in Russia would undermined democratic development there, and that is indeed what happened."

Here is another account by another economist, Michael Hudson, President of the Institute for the Study of Long Term Economic Trends: "The IMF and World Bank wiped out Russian savers with a hyper inflation by getting rid of all the capital controls and letting the rouble float. So it was just one bad advice after another and now the Russians realize they've been taken. And they're trying to figure out how on earth do we get out of this mess following the West's advice.

They thought, and the Baltics thought, that they were being told how to develop in the way that the West did. Neo-liberalism is the exact opposite of how Britain and the United States, Germany, Japan, and now China, got rich-by progressive taxation, and having public infrastructure provided at much lower cost than privatized infrastructure and a resource fund tax, basically a land tax which is how Europe and America – states and localities – have been financed all throughout their history."

Am I crazy, or did the West act in a way that resulted in a large number of deaths and shortened lifespans and desperate poverty? Well, maybe not. OK, let's go back to the re unification of Germany and the breakup of the Soviet Union:

I want to quote from an article from the Los Angeles Times dated 5/20/16 titled: "Russia's got a point: The U.S. broke a NATO promise"

"(Leaders in Moscow) (claim the United States has failed to uphold a promise that NATO would not expand into Eastern Europe, a deal made during the 1990 negotiations between the West and the Soviet Union over German unification." "The West has vigorously protested that no such deal was ever struck. However, hundreds of memos, meeting minutes and transcripts from U.S. archives indicate otherwise."

So what the Los Angeles Times is saying then is that the West has been very dishonest in this matter.

In my humble opinion, the Los Angeles Times should seriously reconsider the frame of reference taken in their reporting on Russia. To help fuel a conflict may be good news for NBC and CBS (who are owned by groupings of companies that also include the arms industry), and fueling conflict may be good news for the defense agencies that will get more funding and better career opportunities, but it is bad news for everybody else, the normal people, who are concerned about other issues, more humble things that pertain to the ideas of nuclear winter and mutually assured destruction.

The people want to live in peace and mutual prosperity, which in turn, is an existential threat to the Pentagon and to the professional trained liars at the CIA and other secretive agencies. By telling only half the story, The Times is working on the wrong side – the dark side.

With what I have written in this article, I have just provided you with all the information that you need in order to become an advocate for peace. Let's see what happens next in the Time's reporting. The whole world needs your help.

So that is the end of the re print from that book. Now back to the article from Foreign Affairs.

On the bottom of page 123: *"The United States central objective should be to keep large states in both regions from gaining so much influence as to shift the local balance of power in their favor"*. I believe that this was the idea behind the previous efforts against Russia in the past, and I believe this applies to U.S. behavior towards Iran as well. Unfortunately, this type of strategy, keeping other countries down, has a down side, and the down side is that it is evil.

The United States cannot attain to being a great nation by preventing other nations from growing strong. That is very faulty thinking.

1. It causes poverty in other nations.
2. It means that the U.S. is then directly responsible for causing that poverty in other nations.
3. It creates the need for precious resources to be squandered on too much "national security".
4. That causes poverty in the U.S., as resources are diminished for programs that stimulate the U.S. economy, such as wide availability of higher education, a safe and effective infrastructure for commerce, and a healthy population well served by an effective and abundantly available health care, ready to provide first rate service to the national economy.
5. It creates enemies. Example: "a vindictive Russia".

6. It draws attention and resources away from solving national and international problems, such as global warming.
7. It fools nobody and people around the world see the U.S. as a pariah state. A large international poll in January of 2014 found that the U.S. is considered around the world as the greatest threat to world peace.
8. We already have much of the North American continent. That's a lot. Why not care for it?
9. There are 2 real existential threats today. Not China and Russia, Global Warming and accidental nuclear war. On nuclear proliferation, we must meet the challenge through diplomacy, arms reduction treaties, peaceful co-existence, proving to other powers that we are of good will. On global warming, we need to respond with a war like effort to radically change to renewable energy, if we are to survive. Science tells us we have 11 years as of the date of this writing, December 2019, if we are to survive as a species.
10. We cannot afford to police the world. Our deficits will grow to such extremes as they already are, that the internationally recognized value of the dollar will crash, and take the whole U.S. economy with it. This same article states that the current national debt is 23 trillion dollars.
11. This is a prescription for war against countries that are armed with nuclear weapons. The problem here is identical to the global warming problem – science/reality. In this case, nuclear winter.

Even a "small" nuclear war between India and Pakistan using perhaps only 100 nuclear bombs would not only cause a nuclear winter, but at the same time it would dissolve the atmosphere's ozone layer. So it is in the interest of our national security that India and Pakistan find a peaceful solution to the Kashmir issue.

It is too late for these strategies mentioned in this article, and they are not only evil, but reckless. In other words, Elbridge A Colby, former U.S. Deputy Assistant Secretary of Defense, and A. Wess Mitchell, former U.S. Assistant Secretary of State for European & Eurasian affairs, are a couple of damn fools, if you know what I mean.

The authors state: *"Engaging in a war with Iran, sustaining a large military presence in Afghanistan, or intervening in Venezuela, as some in the administration want to do, is antithetical to success in a world of great power competition."* Let's say that I totally agree with that statement.

The authors note: *"This is only the beginning of what is likely to be a decades-long effort"* and *"The United States then, must prepare for a generational effort."* While once again, science gives humanity 11 years to radically change course on the use of fossil fuels. So we don't even have time for this discussion – that is, if science matters.

The authors note: *"More change is needed to deter future attempts by Russia to create faits accomplish along its border" "in particular, the United States needs forces that can deploy quickly enough to contest any Russian land grab from the outset"* In other words, surround Russia with military bases. Yet Russia is the nation with the largest land mass of any nation on the planet and their population is only just under half that of the United States. They don't need more land, they need security. Therefore, to prevent any land grabs from *Russia, NATO must withdraw so that Russia can feel safe.* Then there will be a greater chance of peace, except for one thing – the Pentagon will have to get smaller, which will allow the American people to live better lives, due to the freeing up of hundreds of billions of dollars every year, to be used for human betterment.

In fact, a 2017 publication from the Defense Intelligence Agency titled: "Russia Military Power" is quite revealing. An excerpt from the chapter on Military Doctrine & Strategy reads as follows:

"Moscow seeks to promote a multi-polar world predicated on the principles of respect for state sovereignty and non-interference in other states internal affairs, the primacy of the United Nations, and a careful balance of power preventing one state or a group of states from dominating the international order." "Moscow has sought to build a robust military able to project power, add credibility to Russian diplomacy, and ensure that Russian interests can no longer be summarily dismissed without consequence."

So that's how the Pentagon sees Russia

On page 128: *"Extensive integration with the Chinese economy is necessary for all states, but they must limit Bejing's ability to turn that exposure into coercive leverage."* That is a good point. Look for example at what the U.S. is doing to other nations with their sanctions, and look at what the WTO and IMF are doing to governments around the world.

On page 129: *"The United States should strengthen NATO's deterrent against Russia")("while using sanctions to punish Russian aggressive actions in places such as Syria and Ukrane)"* The authors seem to have somehow forgotten, in their anti-Russian craze, that the Syrian government invited Russia to help them fight the ISIS invaders. What an amazing "mistake" by these high level ex government officials. And the situation in Ukraine was discussed earlier, although there is more to that story.

Much has been written about Russian aggression in Ukraine. But curiously, a lot of important details seem to be left out of the discussion. It turns out that in 2013, the National Endowment for Democracy (NED) which the founding director explained, performs certain functions that had previously been performed by the CIA, had spent millions of dollars on 65 different projects in Ukraine.

Neoliberalism was being promoted. Neoliberalism is a doctrine of laissez-faire economic policies which strives to minimize the role of government. Economist Michael Hudson wrote that one way of describing these policies is to say that they favor creditors.

When government is removed as the equalizing force, the big fish eat the little fish and we end up with monopoly capitalism. The giant corporations (many of which are CFR members and many corporate board members are CFR members) become the de facto government.

Neoliberalism strives to break down trade and finance barriers between nations that have served as protective barriers, through multi-lateral organizations – the WTO, IMF and World Bank, allowing major corporations to operate in countries that have no worker or environmental protections, with the lowest wages, and workers around the world are forced to compete with this arrangement, standing alone without the support of their governments.

One estimate notes that large corporations control approximately 50% of all the wealth on this planet. So by following this race to the bottom, this creates a downward pressure on wages on a worldwide basis.

Lower wages results in sluggish national economic performance due to the public becoming less able to buy the products that they make. These policies at the same time also serve to enhance inequality.

The NED tried, with much success, to convince Ukrainians that the way to national development is through neoliberal policies, whereas neoliberal policies are designed to funnel money to major corporations, at working peoples' expense. Note also that there are ten CFR members serving on the NED board of directors.

In November of 2013, president Yanukovich looked at economic association treaties from Russia and the neoliberal formulations from the EU and he decided that the Russian economic association treaty had more to offer the people of Ukraine. A cover story in German's Spiegel magazine dated 11/24/14 noted in passing that the EU's offer to Ukraine would have cost Ukraine 160 billion dollars. See Global Research, the Canadian Website. The article titled "The $160 billion cost: Why Ukraine's Victor Yanukovych Spurned EU's offer on 20 Nov. 2013"

This decision was followed by violent anti-government demonstrations. Remember that NED had 65 projects active in Ukraine, and between 1991 to 2013, an excess of 5 billion dollars was spent by the U.S. Government to influence public opinion in Ukraine, trying to break that country away from their close ties with Russia.

In February of 2014 there was a successful coup in Ukraine by a group that was anti-Russian. A telephone conversation that was hacked and broadcast by the Russian government revealed that the US State Dept. official and CRF connected Victoria Nuland was explaining to someone that Yatsenyuk should be the next president of Ukraine. Miraculously, Yatsenyuk did become the next president of Ukraine. What a coincidence.

Another interesting article on that Canadian website Global Research is titled "Washington Was Behind Ukraine Coup: Obama Admits That US "Brokered A Deal" in support of "Regime Change"." And that article not only noted what Obama had told CNN regarding brokering a deal, but also noted: "Following the transition of power, Kiev forces launched a military operation against those who refused to recognize the legitimacy of the new government." Note that the voters in the eastern Russian speaking part of Ukraine had voted 90% in favor of Yanucovich .

Only an extremely partisan point of view will blame Russia for any kind of response to this coup that took place on their border.

International law professor at the University of Illinois College of Law, Francis Boyle claimed that Obama was ignorant of the Minsk agreements and of Putin's proposals for peaceful negotiation. Boyle also noted "How can Russia tolerate this gang of Nazis in Kiev setting up shop right there on the borders of Russia, and being armed, equipped and supplied by NATO?" "Of course Russia cannot tolerate that." Boyle went on to express that the U.S. government would not tolerate a coup by an anti U.S. group on their border either, by people with Nazi backgrounds. But then, Boyle is not a member of the Council on Foreign Relations.

Chapter 5

On: The New Intervention Delusion; Nov/Dec 2019 issue, page 84-98 by Richard Fontaine.

Richard Fontaine is reported as the CEO of the Center for a New American Security, who has worked for the State Department, at the National Security Council, and as a foreign policy advisor for Senator John McCain. These are very impressive credential, although in spite of it,

This article contains very serious mis-representations concerning four major events:

1. The war in Syria
2. The war in Afghanistan
3. The war in Libya
4. The war in Yugoslavia.

On the middle of page 93 in the Nov/Dec 2019 edition, "The second Iraq war was supposed to finish the job – but it showed how a purportedly short conflict can lead to an indefinite occupation. To prevent that from happening in Libya, Obama decided to use air power to help oust Qaddafi, but keep American boots off the ground."

What was curiously left out of this discussion can best be described in part of a CNN report by Angela Dewan, dated 9/14/16 titled: "Britains's Libya Intervention led to growth of ISIS, inquiry finds" It turns out that the Parliamentary Foreign Affairs Committee of the British House of Commons found that Britain's part in the military intervention in Libya was based on inaccurate intelligence and erroneous assumptions. The committee found that the British government "failed to identify that the threat to civilians was overstated and that the rebels included a significant Islamist threat."

Note that an Amnesty International investigation in June of 2011 was not able to corroborate allegations of mass human rights violations by Gaddafi regime troops, and instead uncovered evidence of false claims and false statements by rebels in Benghazi.

The Amnesty International investigation also noted how Western media reporting had described the rebels as peaceful and had repeatedly suggested that government forces were committing human rights violations. They called it one-sided reporting.

"The Libyan government was in fact fighting Islamic terrorists." Global Research, a Canadian news organization reported in an article dated 9/23/19 titled: "Libya War was Based on Lies, Bogus Intelligence, NATO Supported and Armed the Rebels." The article also mentions that the Hindustani Times had spoken with Bruce Riedel, a former CIA officer and terrorism expert, who explained that there was an Al Quaeda group operating in Libya, centered in Benghazi.

On page 88, the article reads: "The civil wars in Libya, Syria and Yemen may be tragic, but they do not demand a U.S. military response". The information above seeks to explain, among other things, that what happened in Libya was not a civil war, and the discussion below on Syria also shows that this was also not a civil war either. Note the article below:

Former French Foreign Minister: The War against Syria was Planned Two years before "The Arab Spring"

By Gearóid Ó Colmáin
Global Research, June 15, 2013

In an interview with the French TV station LCP, former French minister for Foreign Affairs Roland Dumas said:

'' I'm going to tell you something. I was in England two years before the violence in Syria on other business. I met with top British officials, who confessed to me that they were preparing something in Syria.

This was in Britain not in America. Britain was organizing an invasion of rebels into Syria. They even asked me, although I was no longer minister for foreign affairs, if I would like to participate.

Naturally, I refused, I said I'm French, that doesn't interest me.''

Getting back to the Foreign Affairs article, on page 96 it discusses circumstances where military action would be justified according to the author. The war in Afghanistan is mentioned as an action which would be justified. "The 2001 decision to attack Al Quaeda and the Taliban in Afghanistan would have met the mark."

Marjorie Cohn, professor of International Law, in a 2008 article entitled "Afghanistan: The other Illegal War" pointed out that under the U.N. Charter, disputes among U.N. members are to be brought to the U.N. Security Council which alone has the authority to authorize the use of force. By not going to the Security Council, the U.S. was in violation of international law when they attacked Afghanistan.

There are two exceptions to this rule. The first exception is if your country is attacked by another nation. A country may respond in self defense – however, Afghanistan did not attack the U.S., 19 people did, and none of them were from Afghanistan.

The second exception is when a nation has certain knowledge that an attack is imminent and that there is not going to be sufficient time to appeal to the Security Council. Although the U.S. claimed that their actions were necessary to prevent another attack, the need to attack Afghanistan was not urgent, as illustrated by the fact that the invasion did not take place until close to one month after the 9/11 event.

The U.N. Security Council generated resolution 1373 to freeze assets, criminalize support of the terrorists, and exchange police information. They did not mention making war on Afghanistan, but in spite of that, President Obama, in his 2/1/9 speech at West Point, said: The United Nations Security Council endorsed the use of all necessary steps to respond to the 9/11 attacks."

The U.N. Charter is a treaty ratified by the U.S., and under article VI of the U.S. Constitution, any treaty ratified by the U.S. is part of the "supreme law of the land". Therefore, the war against Afghanistan is illegal based on United States law.

The invasion of Afghanistan was supposed to have been necessary because the Taliban, who were ruling Afghanistan, had refused to hand over Bin Laden to U.S. Authorities. That is not exactly true. Ten days after the 9/11 attacks CNN reported that the Taliban refused to hand over Bin Laden WITHOUT EVIDENCE. The Taliban noted that Bin Laden had said that he was innocent, so they wanted evidence. But Bush said that "the demands were not open to negotiation or discussion".

After the bombing began in October, the Taliban offered to turn Bin Laden over to a third country, so long as the U.S. could just provide some evidence that he was involved in the 9/11 tragedy, but Bush stated "There's no need to discuss innocence or guilt. We know he's guilty."

So on this basis, I question the author's belief that the war in Afghanistan was in any way justified. On page 97, the war in Syria is noted as a positive example of U.S. intervention;

"ironically, it is the counter ISIS mission in Syria – the one that so frequently elicits calls for its end – that provides a reasonably successful example of how U.S. military intervention can work in practice."

On page 91 towards the bottom, the author warns against withdrawing prematurely from terrorist safe havens such as Syria, yet on page 97 the article continues by discussing special operations: "The operation has banished Iran, Russia, and Syrian government forces from a third of the country". Note that the Syrian government had invited Russia and Iran to assist in the fight against Islamicist forces that had invaded Syria, and it was this group that was responsible for the vast majority of successes against the Al Quaeda and Al Nusra terrorists.

Regarding Syria, and for the purpose of this article, Libya as well, it would be relevant to quote General Wesley Clark, who was the Supreme Allied Commander of NATO from 1997 to 2000, and was commander of the NATO forces in the Kosovo war. On page 130 of his book "Winning Modern Wars" General Clark wrote:

"As I went back through the Pentagon in November 2001, one of the senior military staff officers had time for chat. Yes, we were still on track for going against Iraq, he said. But there was more. This was being discussed as part of a five year campaign plan, he said, and there were a total of seven countries, beginning with Iraq, then Syria, Lebanon, Libya, Iran, Somalia and Sudan." "I left the Pentagon that afternoon deeply concerned."

In a 3/17/19 article by Michel Chussodovsky on the Global Research web page from Canada, in the article titled "It Started in Daraa on March 17, 2011", "The US-NATO-Israel agenda consisted in supporting an Al Quaeda affiliated insurgency integrated by death squads and professional snipers. President Bashar al Assad is then to be blamed for killing his own people."

And there are several sources which express this view. For example, there are 25 colleges and Universities affiliated with a media studies program in the U.S. called Project Censored. Project Censored publishes a book every year and have done so for the past 40 years, which contain what they call the top 25 censored stories of the year. In their 2017 book on page 63, they reported the following:

"In 2011-2012, after Syrian President Bashar al Assad refused to cooperate with Turkey's proposal to create a natural gas pipeline between Qatar and Turkey through Syria, Turkey and its allies became "the major architects of Syria's Civil War." "In 2012, the U.S., U.K., France,

Qatar and Saudi Arabia, along with Turkey began to organize, arm, and finance rebels to form the Free Syrian Army, consistent with long-standing U.S. plans to destabilize Syria.

Suggested reading on this subject would be "The Dirty War on Syria" by Tim Anderson, and Voices from Syria" by Mark Taliano.

Back to the article by Richard Fontain. On page 85, I quote: "despite the well known failures of recent large scale interventions, there is also a record of more successful ones – including the effort today in Syria"

I would like to add to that, According to Human Rights Watch, the estimated death toll since the start of the war through March of 2018 is 511,000 people. According to the United Nations High Commissioner for Refugees (UNHCR) 6.6 million people have been displaced inside Syria, and another 5.6 million Syrian refugees can be found outside of Syria.

The references listed above, Professor Michel Chussodovsky, Mark Taliano and Tim Anderson provide a large trove of evidence that discredits claims of random senseless violence perpetrated by the Assad government against the Syrian people.

Regarding the use of chemical weapons, in an article by the Los Angeles Times, "Fact finding teams from the Organization for the Prohibition of Chemical Weapons, an international watchdog agency based in the Hague were expected to arrive in Douma on Saturday to collect evidence on the April 7th attack that left 43 people dead." However, the U.S. bombed the city a day before they arrived to do their investigation. This was at a time when the U.S. Centcom chief General Votel told Lindsey Graham that the Syrian Government has won this war.

The historical backdrop is as follows; Obama had threatened Assad with retaliation and regime change if he were to use chemical weapons. With this background, along with the fact that Syria had essentially won the war, what possible motive could Assad have had for using chemical weapons? To add to this, in 2019 Reporter Max Blumenthal reported that the U.S. government is blocking Syria from importing building materials for Syria to rebuild their country. This was on you-tube '"Redacted VIP, 174" So hopefully this added data can help to add more pieces to this puzzle.

Furthermore, in a 12/14/19 article in England's newspaper the Daily Mail, which has more than 10 million readers, see the article titled: "Peter Hitchens reveals fresh evidence that UN watchdog suppressed report casting doubt on Assad gas attack." The article explains that a senior official at the Organization for Prohibition of Chemical Weapons (OPCW) demanded the removal of all traces of a document which undermined claims that gas cylinders had been dropped from the air – their so called evidence that the Syrian government was responsible.

Also, see the article by Global Research, also dated 12/14/19 titled: "New Wikileaks Bombshell: 20 inspectors dissent from Syria Chemical Attack Narrative. Leaked Documents and e-mails of OPCW" The articles show that there was no gas attack by the Syrian government against people in Douma in April of 2018.

On page 84 of Fontain's article: "Although the precise financial cost depends on how one counts, what is certain is that more than 4,500 U.S. military personnel have been killed in Iraq and nearly 2,500 in Afghanistan, plus tens of thousands injured in both wars – to say nothing of the casualties among allied forces, military contractors and local civilians.

In regards to civilian casualties in Iraq, I refer to a 3/19/18 article from Alternet titled: "The Staggering Death Toll in Iraq". They looked at the 2006 report by the Lancet medical journal, which British government officials privately admitted was "likely to be right" and then looked at the 2007 study done by the British polling firm Opinion Research Business (ORB) along with work done by the organization Just Policy which continued the count after the 2007 ORB study to bring it up to early 2018. The result was 2.4 million Iraqis were killed since 2003, with a minimum of 1.5 million and a maximum of 3.4 million. So I think that type of information is missing from this article.

On page 93 "But because Saddam was left in power, the Iraq problem festered." Mr Fontaine did not explain what this "Iraq problem" was, but I can say that due to heavy sanctions, Iraq was not allowed to expand their oil industry. In anticipation of eventual lifting of sanctions, Saddam had communicated with several different companies to assist with oil extraction, however none of those companies were American companies. Secondly, Saddam had plans to change his reserve currency out of dollars and use Euros instead. Several analysts believe that this was the reason that the U.S. forcibly removed him and executed him.

Kaddafi of Libya was communicating with several African countries about starting a new currency based on gold. He also reportedly wanted to use France as Libya's main Western country to have relations with. There are many analysts that believe that these are the reasons that Kaddafi was forcibly removed and ultimately executed.

Regarding the invasion of Afghanistan, in an article by David Ray Griffin titled: "The Invasion of Afghanistan, October 7, 2001: Did 9/11 Justify the War in Afghanistan?", the analyst wrote that the Bush

Administration had a 4 day meeting with the Taliban in Berlin in July 2001. The U.S. government had demanded that the Taliban create a government of "national unity" by sharing power with factions friendly to the United States". This was in order to create a situation of "stability" so that Unocal could be able to build a pipeline that would transport oil and natural gas from the Caspian Sea region to the Indian Ocean through Afghanistan and Pakistan and that this pipeline would be secure.

In the 2002 book by Brisard and Dasquie titled "Forbidden Truth: U.S. - Taliban Secret Oil Diplomacy", on page 43, they wrote that in that meeting in Berlin, the U.S. representative reportedly stated: "Either you accept our offer of a carpet of gold or we bury you under a carpet of bombs." The Taliban rejected this offer, and reportedly, the U.S. had already decided two months prior to 9/11 to invade Afghanistan. Afghanistan can also serve as an outpost near both Russia and China, and the U.S. military, with its 800+ military bases located outside the borders of the United States, is always looking for more real estate.

On page 88 I quote: "Successive presidents have used military might to prevent, halt, or punish mass atrocities – Clinton to cease the genocide against Bosnian Muslims in the Balkan," O.K., but that is not what happened.

In October 17,1999, Stratfor, a company involved in global intelligence and who contracts with the United States Government wrote the following: "Where Are Kosovo's Killing Fields?" was the title of their article. The article begins as follows:

"During its four month war against Yugoslavia, NATO argued that Kosovo was a land wracked by mass murder; official estimates indicated that some 10,000 ethnic Albanians were killed in a Serb rampage of ethnic clensing. Yet four months into an international investigation bodies numbering only in the hundreds have been exhumed." "(evidence of mass murder has not yet materialized on the scale to justify the war."). ("the central justification for war was that only intervention would prevent the slaughter of Kosovo's ethnic Albanian population.") "But the aftermath of the war has brought precious little evidence, despite the entry of Western forensics teams searching for evidence of war crimes. Mass murder is difficult to hide."

In an article by Michael Parenti titled "The Rational Destruction of Yugoslavia" (www.MichaelParenti.Org) he notes "experts in surveillance photography and wartime propaganda charged NATO with running a propaganda campaign on Kosovo that lacked any supporting evidence. State Department reports of mass graves and of 100,000 to 500,000 missing Albanian men "are just ludicrous", according to these independent critics. He then references an article by the San Francisco Chronicle by Charles Radin and Louise Palmer titled " Experts Voice Doubts on Claims of Genocide: Little Evidence for NATO Assertions" 4/22/1999.

The German Foreign Office is quoted: "Even in Kosovo, an explicit political persecution linked to Albanian ethnicity is not verifiable...The actions of the (Yugoslav) security forces (were) not directed against the Kosovo-Albanians as an ethnically defined group, but against the military opponent and its actual or alleged supporters.

Parenti identifies the NATO political leaders as the biggest war criminals, pointing out the immense damage that occurred due to the long bombing campaign. The charter of NATO provides that NATO can take military action only in response to aggression committed against one of its members, but Yugoslavia had not attacked any member country of NATO, so the war was waged by NATO in violation of NATO's own charter.

I would like to quote from the portion of Parenti's article wherein he provides his explanation of NATO's motive behind this war in Yugoslavia:

"When the productive social capital of any part of the world is obliterated, the potential value of private capital elsewhere is enhanced — especially when the crisis faced today by western capitalism is one of overcapacity. Every agricultural base destroyed by western aerial attacks (as in Iraq) or by NAFTA and GATT (as in Mexico and elsewhere), diminishes the potential competition and increases the market opportunities for multinational corporate agribusiness. To destroy publicly-run Yugoslav factories that produced auto parts, appliances, or fertilizer — or a publicly financed Sudanese plant that produced pharmaceuticals at prices substantially below their western competitors — is to enhance the investment value of western producers. And every television or radio station closed down by NATO troops or blown up by NATO bombs extends the monopolizing dominance of the western media cartels. The aerial destruction of Yugoslavia's social capital served that purpose."

Nato started bombing Yugoslavia on 3/24/1999. In the late 1960's and 1970's Yugoslavia took out foreign loans to expand the Yugoslavia's industrial base. Eventually, the IMF demanded restructuring and an austerity program. In 1991 Congress passed the Foreign Operations Appropriations Act. This act provided that any part of Yugoslavia failing to declare independence within six months would lose U.S. financial support. The law also demanded separate elections in each of the six Yugoslav republics and mandated U.S. State Department approval of not only the election procedures but also the results. Aid would only go to separate republics, not to the

Yugoslavia government. The idea to split up Yugoslavia originated in the United States. It was not an idea which originated in Yugoslavia. The NATO bombing began in March of 1999, about eight years after the passage of the Foreign Operations Appropriations Act.

Chapter 6 – The two Venezuelas

In 1975 a young Canadian economist, Michel Chussodovsky was hired by the Venezuelan government's planning department for a temporary position. Chussodovsky performed a country wide study on poverty. Just before he was ready to release the report, he couldn't believe the results of his own study. A quote: "I contacted my friend (medical doctor) at the University who specialized in nutrition and said, "This seems horrendously high." His response was "No, you're absolutely on.""

He distributed his report to several government department heads, only to find that his report had been confiscated by the planning department. Although they agreed with the report, they felt that it was too inflammatory to circulate this report, which revealed the fact that more than 70% of the entire population of Venezuela was not even getting enough food to eat.

Three years later in 1978, Chussodovsky published his report which had been censored, in a book titled: "La Miseria en Venezuela" (The Misery in Venezuela) and it became widely circulated and used in schools and Universities there.

He found that more than 70% of the population were not able to meet minimum calorie & protein requirements, while about 45% were suffering from extreme malnutrition. One in four children had never been to school. More than half of school age children never entered high school. There was no access to health care for the majority of the population. And more.

This data was based on the 1970's but the 1980's were far worse because of hyperinflation, which this economist attributed to the conditions imposed by the IMF.

In 1975 the oil industry was nationalized by law, but the Venezuelan government was still not receiving the benefits which instead, were still benefiting the foreign oil companies.

Chussodovsky: "Ironically, I was asked to draft a text which was to be used for the oil nationalization speech, which was a very important document, because it defined what you are going to do with the oil. I drafted an analysis of this, essentially saying the following: That the oil revenues would be recycled to a societal project alleviating poverty. It was explained conceptually that the oil money now belongs to the country and not to the oil companies, and consequently this is the avenue that we choose."

In 2014 a new book came out titled: "Venezuela Before Chavez, Anatomy of an Economic Collapse" published by Richard Hausman & Francisco Rodriguez. The book includes contributions from 19 authors who explain how a country that became rich by 1970, went into a steady collapse during a 23 year period from 1978 – 2001, before Chavez became president.

Foreign Affairs has put out a collection of 8 articles on Venezuela titled: The Collapse of Venezuela. I have read 5 of them and aside from the article reproduced from 1960 (I thought that was odd to pull out something that dated), the articles are all from the opposition camp opposing the Chavez/Maduro governments. I will sample and respond to several points from two of the articles and then do my best to explain what I see is the true motivation for the creation of this material.

The one page introduction to this anthology starts out with: *How did things go wrong in Venezuela? In the 1970's it was the wealthiest country in South America; oil profits were flowing in, and Venezuela was the host, not the source, of the region's refugees.* So they started with 1970 and jumped immediately to today, with Venzuela under major U.S. scanctions, without mentioning the 23 year slide mentioned above, prior to Chavez and Maduro!!!

The article continues with: *"Roughly 90 percent of the population now lives below the poverty line."* (no reference is provided – no proof.) *"Food and basic medicines are often unavailable or too expensive for all but a small elite") ("more than four million Venezuelans have fled their homes"),* - **but no mention is made about the U.S. sanctions.**

In respect to the U.S. sanctions on the Venezuelan economy, I will simply quote some newspaper article headlines in order to demonstrate precisely what the intro had failed to mention:

BBC News, 8/9/19: "U.S. sanctions may worsen Venezuela Suffering, says UN rights chief"

New York Times 2/8/19: "U.S. Sanctions Are Aimed at Venezuela's Oil. Its Citizens May Suffer First"

The Independent 4/26/19: "U.S. Sanctions on Venezuela responsible for "tens of thousands" of deaths, claims new report"

Telesur English: " U.N. Human Rights Council Adopts Resolution Rejecting US Sanctions"

Wall Street Journal 1/28/19: "U.S. Imposes Sanctions on Venezuela's Oil Industry"

The Wall Street Journal article states: "The sanctions on Petroleos de Venezuela SA, The South American country's main exporter, are the culmination of a two year pressure campaign, and are an attempt to funnel income from the country's biggest revenue generator into the hands of opposition leader Juan Guaido."
Notice that the January 2019 article says that this is the culmination of a two year pressure campaign!

So the intro failed to mention this. The article continues:

January 23, 2019, at first seemed like **a turning point** *(emphasis added) Juan Guaido, an opposition politician who was the leader of Venezuela's National Assembly, declared Nicolas Maduro's presidency unlawful and named himself interim president.*

How on earth would that be a turning point? Imagine someone in the position of Nancy Pelosi declaring themselves president when they did not even run for the position. That of course would corrupt the whole system. The current president of Venezuela was democratically elected, so look at what is being promoted here. These are clearly not American values. In America we value democracy, but in Foreign Affairs magazine – apparently not, or not always so.

The intro goes on to say that eventually many foreign governments recognized Guido, but it failed to mention that the vast majority of foreign nations, about 150 of them, did **not** recognize Guido and did not agree with a person who didn't even run, proclaiming themself as president of a country that already has a democratically elected president. This phenomenon of a number of states agreeing with this would be an extremely important and revealing study on foreign relations and power relations between the U.S. and various other nations, but the article does not address that.

The intro continues as follows: *"Finally, we explore the reasons for the current deadlock – why, even as Venezuela teeters on the brink of total collapse, Maduro and his generals have so far maintained a grip on the country that neither opposition protest nor foreign pressure can shake."*

Why is Venezuela being described as on the brink of total collapse? Because of the sanctions of course – yet the sanctions are not even mentioned. Speaking of how "Maduro and his generals have so far maintained a grip on the country " this statement very clearly suggests that Venezuela is a military dictatorship. Venezuela is not a military dictatorship, so the intro is completely dishonest and quite misleading. What that means in layman's terms is that they are liars.

Furthermore, regarding that grip on the country that is currently unshakeable, note that in Venezuela, just like in the United States, France, Canada, and Germany, the armed forces support their president. But the proper explanation as to the reason why Maduro is the president of his country is explained by the fact that Maduro won reelection with 67.7% of the vote. In the United States you would have to go back to the 1972 election where Nixon was elected with 60% of the vote in order to get anywhere comparable in the United States to Maduro's popularity in Venezuela, and it's safe to say that Nixon's generals were behind him too.

A March 12, 2018 article by Reuters noted that Maduro had asked the United Nations to send election observers to the upcoming election, - and the Venezuelan opposition asked the U.N. not to send observers! That would tend to suggest then that it is not Maduro who is crooked, but instead, the opposition. And Foreign Affairs Magazine is without a doubt a part of this crooked opposition.

I will quote from a 5/29/18 article by Counterpunch: "More than 300 international representatives from organizations such as the African Union, the Caribbean Community and the Electoral Experts Council of Latin America, as well as former heads of states, parliamentarians, trade unionists and solidarity activists, were present for Venezuela's May 20 presidential vote." Note that the Council of Electoral Experts of Latin America is comprised of top electoral officials from throughout the region.

And they certified the election.

The Carter Center received a Nobel prize for their work observing elections. Ex U.S. President Jimmy Carter, who won that Nobel prize and knew what he was talking about, said "As a matter of fact, of the 92 elections that we've monitored, I would say the election process in Venezuela is the best in the world".

So all of the above is my response to just the one page introduction to this anthology.

Now I would like to take a look at article number 5 by Franciso Rodriguez from the March/April 2008 edition, "An Empty Revolution". Note that Hugo Chavez was first elected President of Venezuela ten years before this article had been written, in 1998.

This author points out: "Neither official statistics nor independent estimates show any evidence that Chavez has reoriented state priorities to benefit the poor." Five pages later on in this same article, he explains: "The average share of the budget devoted to health, education, and housing under Chavez in his first eight years in office was 25.12%, essentially identical to the average share of 25.08 percent in the previous eight years." **However – the same article says that government expenditures are now 29.49% of GDP, up from 18.8% in 1999.** So, that's the same 25% figure of what is now a pie that represents 29.49% of GDP instead of 18.8%. So this author is either very dishonest, or he needs to go back to grammar school. I don't' think that the author needs to go back to grammar school, so I'll say instead that he is a liar.

Chavez's critics are saying that he is a socialist, and socialism does not work. He has increased government spending as a percentage of GDP up to almost 30%. Comparisons are often helpful in providing a needed perspective. In 2011, Chris Edwards of the Cato institute reported that according to his study the U.S. government (Federal State and Local combined) spends 41% of the U.S. GDP. One analysis projects 36.3% for 2020 for the U.S. The E.U. reported 46.2% in 2017. So the U.S. and Europe apparently then are much more socialist than Venezuela. If we are trying desperately to save Venezuela from the evils of socialism, then shouldn't we attack ourselves first, and worry about dear Venezuela later?

In a different part of the article, Rodriguez says "through a combination of luck and manipulation of the political system, Chavez has faced elections at times of strong economic growth". So Rodriguez is suggesting or saying that Chavez manipulates the system to have elections during times of economic growth. That is not possible because elections are held at regular intervals by law. The president is not allowed to change election dates and does not change them. So this is - another lie, -of course.

Rodriguez states the following:

"The real question is thus not whether poverty has fallen but whether the Chavez government has been particularly effective at converting this period of economic growth into

poverty reduction. One way to evaluate this is by calculating the reduction in poverty for every percentage point increase in per capita income – in economist's lingo, the income elasticity of poverty reduction. This calculation shows an average reduction of one percentage point in poverty for every percentage point in per capita GDP growth during this recovery, a ratio that compares unfavorably with those of many other developing countries, for which studies tend to put the figure at around two percentage points."

I'm not an economist, but this doesn't appear to be a valid approach. For example, if the starting point for per capita income is extremely low, and if you go from making, say $3.00 per day up to $3.30 per day, that is a 10% increase – but it still would remain a picture of extreme poverty. Also, this approach doesn't take inequality into account. In the U.S. as an example, over the last 30 years, the U.S. saw a tremendous increase in GDP, but it all pretty much went to the wealthy, and most peoples' wages stayed exactly the same, but the poor actually saw a small decrease in earnings. Of course the U.S. might be considered a bad example because they have the highest rate of inequality in the developed world.

"Similarly, one would expect pro-poor growth to be accompanied by a marked decrease in income inequality. But according to the Venezuelan Central Bank, inequality has actually increased during the Chavez administration, with the Gini coefficient increasing from 0.44 to 0.48 between 2000 and 2005."

But a 12/14/2012 article by Carles Muntaner, Joan Benach & Maria Paez Victor in Counterpunch titled "The

Achievements of Hugo Chavez" stated that Venezuela is now the country with the lowest Gini coefficient in all of Latin America, and that inequality has been reduced by 54%. In 2014, Nicky Fabianicic, resident U.N. coordinator for Venezuela said that Venezuela was "one of the leading countries in Latin America and the Carribbean in reducing inequality"

So, was the author of this article – lying again?...

"In Venezuela one can see the misiones everywhere: in government posters lining the streets of Caracas, in the ubiquitous red shirts issued to program participants and worn by government supporters at Chavez rallies, in the bloated government budget allocations.   The only place where one will be hard-pressed to find them is in the human development statistics."

That is a good point. What about the human development statistics? The Human development Index of the United Nations Development Program lists Venezuela as #61 out of 176 countries. Venezuela has moved up 7 places in the first ten years under the leadership of Hugo Chavez.

"Even more disappointing are the results of the government's Robinson literacy program." *" In contrast to the government's claim, we found that there were more than one million illiterate Venezuelans by the end of 2005."*

Note that Unesco has recognized that illiteracy has been eliminated in Venezuela during the period of Hugo Chavez as president, and Venezuela is second in Latin America and Fifth in the world with the greatest proportion of University Students per capita. Unicef representative Kiyomi Kawaguchi said that from 2009-2010, 7,700,000 students attended school, an increase of 24% over ten years prior.

Rodriguez writes:

"A survey taken by the Venezuelan polling firm Alfredo Keller & Asociados in September 2007 showed that only 22 percent of Venezuelans think poverty has improved under Chavez, while 50 percent think it has worsened and 27 percent think it has stayed the same."

And then only a few sentences later, he writes:

"In polls, an overwhelming majority have expressed support for Chavez's stewardship of the economy and reported that their personal situation was improving."

So that is exactly contradictory.

Rodriguez writes:

This growing economic crisis is the predictable result of the gross mismanagement of the economy by Chavez's economic team."

So in this 2008 article in Foreign Affairs, he talks about "This growing economic crisis" the result of gross mis management of the economy, yet, an article from the Guardian dated 10/4/12, drawing data from the World Bank, the IMF, Reuters, UNHCR and other agencies, state that GDP per capita has risen from $4,105.00 when Chavez first assumed the presidency, to $10,801.00 by 2011.

Rodrigues writes that as a result of Chavez's policies, *"the response has been a steep drop in food production and widening food scarcity."* Although by 2012, as a result of farm subsidies, Venezuela went from importing 90% of their food in 1980 to importing less than 30% by 2012 because domestic food supply had increased.

Rodriguez writes: *"the government generated an inflationary crisis."* It is true that inflation did increase. From 1999 to 2011, inflation increased from 23.57% up to 26.09%.

Rodriguez writes:

But as we proceeded to meet with officials, the economic crisis was spilling over into the political arena with the opposition calling for street demonstrations in response to Chavez's declining poll numbers. Soon, workers at the state oil company PDVSA joined the protest."

It would be relevant to explain that the National Endowment for Democracy, (the CIA) funded Venezuelan opposition groups with funds eventually totaling more than one hundred million dollars, (according to Eva Golinger a U.S. attorney) and on 4/11/2002 the U.S. staged an unsuccessful coup attempt to overthrow Chavez, the democratically elected president of the Venezuelan people.

Also, to repeat: "opposition calling for street demonstrations in response to Chavez's declining poll numbers." Yet, the 4th sentence in the start of this article, Rodriguez notes that Chavez won his presidential election by 62.8% of the vote. So that's another contradiction, right? When you see these things, the explanation is that the author is lying.

In the article Rodriguez mentions "*a dramatic decline in Venezuela's oil-production capacity*, but in fact, in 1999 Venezuela's oil exports resulted in 14.4 billion dollars in sales, and by 2011, over 60 billion dollars in sales.

Rodriguez wrote: "*I have seen to what extent he has failed to live up to his own promises and Venezuelan's expectations. Now, voters are making the same realization – a realization that will ultimately lead to Chavez's demise.*" What actually happened is that Chavez was re-elected by a strong majority.

Rodriguez wrote: "*Looking back, one persistent question will be how the Venezuelan government has been able to convince so many people of the success of its antipoverty efforts despite the complete absence of real evidence of their effectiveness.*

Good point. "They convinced" Reuters, Opec, the International Monetary Fund, The World Bank, Unicef, The U.S. Energy Information Administration, the United Nations High Commissioner for Refugees, the UN Economic Commission for Latin America, & the Caribbeans, and Oxfam, along with a multitude of reporters, economists and yet other U.N agencies.

I was also going to review the first article in the series by Moises Naim and Francisco Toro, titled: Venezuela's Suicide", but I decided that it would be redundant, as they also tell a lot of stories and they provided absolutely no evidence – no references to back up their claims.

It would also be instructive to point out that Venezuela has a free press. The vast majority of the press is owned by people who are right wing, and they criticize the government freely and openly, making the claim that Chavez is some kind of a dictator, patently absurd. The government accounts for approximately 6.5% of the broadcasting which is far less than Norway, the recognized world leader in freedom of the press.

What are the achievements of Hugo Chavez?

Rahul Shrivastava, works at Ministry of External Affairs, in India, and this is his response to the question; What are the Accomplishments of Hugo Chavez?

Hugo Rafael Chávez Frías, popularly known as Hugo Chavez, was President of Venezuela from 1999 until his death in 2013. Born in a poor working class family, he went on to become the youngest President in Venezuelan history at the age of 44.

During his Presidency, the following happened in Venezuela:

- GDP per capita rose from about US$ 4000 to nearly US$ 11000.

- Unemployment dropped from nearly 15% to about 6%.
- Extreme poverty decreased from 23.4% to 8.5%.
- Infant mortality decreased from 20 per 1000 to 13, the lowest in South America.
- Annual oil exports increased from US$ 14 billion to over US$ 60 billion.
- Venezuela moved up 7 positions in the United Nations Human Development Index.
- The minimum wage increased by more than 600%.
- Free education, including in universities was introduced by Chavez. When Chavez took over, nearly 40% of the population was illiterate. During his Presidency, Venezuela reached 100% literacy rate. Venezuela also became the 6th top country in terms of university enrollment. In less than 3 years, Chavez's educational missions taught 3 million adult Venezuelans how to read and write, completely eliminating illiteracy.
- Chavez introduced the health care programme called Mission Barrio Adentro, sent doctors to isolated communities and covered the entire population of Venezuela. Another health programme Mission Milagro restored eyesight of 300,000 Venezuelans.
- Under Mission Mercal, Chavez set up 8000 subsidized supermarkets and small markets all over the country serving about 8 million Venezuelans every month.
- To transfer power to the people, 35,000 community councils and 130,000 grassroots circles were set up.

After Chavez came to power, Venezuela's name was changed from Republic of Venezuela to the Bolivarian Republic of Venezuela in honor of the liberator of Venezuela, Simon Bolivar. He introduced a new Constitution, which is gender-neutral.

Chavez was the brain behind several regional organizations and institutions in Latin America and the Caribbean. These include: 1) the Community of Latin American and Caribbean States (CELAC) with 33 members. 2) the Union of South American Nations (UNASUR), an integration of 12 South American countries which has a parliament, a presidential forum and a secretariat. 3) the Bolivarian Alliance for the Peoples of Our Americas (ALBA), a trade alliance of 8 countries. 4) Banco del Sur (Bank of the South), a development bank for Latin America. 5) Telesur, a pan-South America television network. 6) PetroSur, a petroleum company with shared ownership of Latin American countries. 7) PetroCaribe, an oil alliance with Caribbean countries for supply of oil from Venezuela at concessional rates.

So this brings us to the next section on Venezuela.

Why all the lies from Foreign Affairs Magazine?

Many years ago, in the run-up to the Iraq war, I signed up for a dish television service. My wife was changing channels and we found a program that we were not familiar with called Democracy Now. A high level operative of the United Nations weapons inspection group, Scott Ritter was being interviewed. He mentioned that his group had been all over Iraq during the course of the last seven years, and that there is absolutely no way that Iraq could be in possession of any meaningful supply of weapons of mass destruction. But he also said another thing that I thought was very important. He mentioned that no television program on any of the major network stations would give him an interview. The interviewer and Scott Ridder thought that it was interesting that so much concern was being expressed in the news about Saddam's weapons of mass destruction and yet, nobody wanted to interview the person who had been one of the people in charge of the U.N. weapons inspection team for a several years.

As we all eventually found out, they were all lying about Iraq. Iraq had no weapons of mass destruction, which had been the rationale given for invading the country.

In the weeks surrounding Colin Powell's famous speech before the United Nations on February 5, 2003, pushing for an invasion of Iraq, "FAIR" Fairness & Accuracy In Reporting – a media watch organization, found and reviewed 393 interviews on the issue of war, in the main stream media. Of those 393 interviews, **only three** were with antiwar guests. So main stream media was actually advocating for war.

Iraq has a very large amount of oil. Saddam Hussein did not want U.S. companies doing business in Iraq, meaning that U.S. oil companies were going to be shut out of doing business in Iraq.

Venezuela has a very large amount of oil too. The Venezuelan government owns and runs the oil industry, meaning that U.S. oil companies are shut out of doing business in Venezuela.

Colin Powell's speech, along with favorable main stream press coverage for war, created a situation whereby the American people would be in less of a position to strongly advocate against such a war. So that pro war press for the war in Iraq is comparable to today's coverage of Venezuela, as exemplified here in Foreign Affairs Magazine.

In addition to oil, Venezuela, like Iraq under Saddam Hussein, has a strong government that is not very open to corporate globalization and penetration by multi-national corporations. This means that in the course of these people in Venezuela going about living their daily lives, our corporations don't make any of their money in the process. If history teaches us anything, this is not a good indicator for longevity of a government.

So in closing this section, there are two Venezuelas, the one that we read about in Foreign Affairs magazine, and in the main stream press for that matter, and then there is the second or other Venezuela, which is a country that goes by the name of Venezuela.

Chapter 7 – An Economic Perspective

It is no accident that WTO rules work against developing countries to the benefit of advanced countries. The rules were formulated by corporate insiders from developed countries, and they remove barriers to trade and the movement of capital. In this type of scenario, all economic activity becomes an open competition with the entire world, and the giant multinational corporations are positioned to win every time against the companies in small developing countries.

Economist Ha Joon Chang, assistant Director of Development Studies at Cambridge University notes that historically speaking, government promotion of infant industries has been the very key to development for most of the developed world. To promote infant industries, governments have to set up protective barriers to free trade.

Here is a quote from Ha Joon Chang's book "Bad Samaritans, discussing Alexander Hamilton, the first Secretary of the Treasury for the United States;

"Hamilton proposed a series of measures to achieve the industrial development of his country, including protective tariffs and import bans; subsidies; export bans on key raw materials; import liberalization of and tariff rebates on industrial inputs; prizes and patents for inventions; regulation of product standards; and development of financial and transportation infrastructures. Although Hamilton rightly cautioned against taking these policies too far, they are, nevertheless, a pretty potent and "heretical" set of policy prescriptions. Were he the finance minister of a developing country today, the IMF and the World Bank would certainly have refused to lend money to his country and would be lobbying for his removal from office." Also: "Hamilton provided the blueprint for U.S. economic policy until the end of the second world war."

The WTO requires nations to remove capital controls, and yet almost all of the developed nations maintained very stringent capital controls from the end of World War II through the 1970's.

There is something called heard behavior in investments. When prospects seem good, foreign financial capital will pour into a developing country, often times creating a bubble, and when people change their minds, there can be an outpouring of capital. This happens all the time, however, in developing countries, where the financial markets are tiny in comparison to Western countries, the outpouring and bursting of bubbles by the sudden withdrawal of foreign capital can cause and has caused national disasters for developing countries. This is why each country must be permitted to protect their own economy, even though Western corporations and the U.S. government may not want them to.

The WTO and IMF promote free trade and laissez faire capitalism, but the advanced nations of the world did precisely the opposite in order to get to where they are today.

The United Nations Conference on Trade & Development (UNCTAD) performed a study which argues that the WTO and World Bank's push to liberalize third world countries has resulted in the destruction of many industries, and an increase in unemployment and lower incomes. The study notes that "Across the board, trade liberalization cannot be a substitute for a trade and industrial policy." Ha Joon Chang from the book "Bad Samaritans":

"Virtually all successful economies, developed and developing, got where they are through selective, strategic integration with the world economy, rather than through unconditional global integration."

The IMF, World Bank and WTO direct developing nations to sell off their government assets and services to private companies and to raise taxes in order to pay off their loans more quickly. Typically, the government assets are sold at fire sale prices to Western Multi-National corporations.

WTO Policies promote foreign direct investment for developing countries by promoting privatization of government services and by not allowing governments to be able to choose to buy local to stimulate the local economy, but a U.N. study (Argosin and Mayer: "Foreign Investments in Developing Countries) shows that domestic investments are often a better generator of jobs, and linkages to other firms, than are investments by foreigners. The UN's industrial development organization, in a report (UNIDO press release, inter press service 11/11/96) noted that "in the final analysis, it is the domestic investment, domestic policies and domestic entrepreneurial skills that are ultimately decisive in industrial development." Also, an Unctad study demonstrated that Foreign Direct Investment is more beneficial when combined with government regulations.

Neoliberal policies favor smaller government with outsourcing of government services, deregulation of all industries, lower taxes on corporations and the wealthy, and free trade. So the role of markets are elevated over government in economic governance, and the private sector is enhanced.

To quote Ha Joon Chang from his book "Kicking Away the Ladder": "The Plain fact is that Neoliberal policy reforms have not been able to deliver their central promise –

namely, economic growth." According to data compiled by the World Bank, during the 1960's and 1970's the world economy experienced an over all growth rate of more than 3% per year, compared with only a 1.4% growth rate from 1980 to 2009 – the Neoliberal period (Bad Samaritans was first copyrighted in 2008). For the developed countries, 1950 to 1973 is often referred to as the Golden Age of Capitalism. According to Ha Joon Chang, most commentators attribute this golden age of capitalism to Keynesianism, welfare states, stricter financial regulations, greater unionization of industries, and in some cases such as in France and Austria, nationalized industries.

After the great depression, economist John Maynard Keynes concluded that the market on its own could not generate sufficient aggregate demand. His idea was to use government programs to uplift the general public and to increase their purchasing power, which would stimulate the economy. Various methods were used such as progressive taxation, jobs programs, massive public works programs, and social programs to fight poverty. These methods worked.

French economist Thomas Picketty, in his book "Capital" performed a 200 year study showing that the rate of the return of capital is greater than the rate of economic growth. What that means or suggests, is that the rich will eventually end up with everything. History past and present validates this, which I believe points us back to Keynesian type policies as the antidote, in a capitalist system.

One of the criticisms of the WTO, IMF and World Bank is that they limit domestic policy options for developing countries which prevents them from pursuing policies to help eradicate poverty. For example, under WTO rules, governments are not even allowed to regulate to ensure that the value of imports vs exports will remain balanced within certain safe ranges. These three organizations have a memorandum of understanding that they will all give the same advice. A report by the World Bank's Chief Economist argued that certain WTO agreements are not economically viable for third world countries, but the World Bank is not permitted to pursue this any further due to their memorandum of understanding.

In the book "Trade For Life" by Mark Curtis, he notes:

"Developed country governments display massive hypocrisy when it comes to trade liberalization. They fail to practice what they preach. They preach that unbridled trade liberalism is in the interests of all. They practice something very different: restricting access to their own markets for the products of most importance to the poor, most notoriously agriculture and textiles. When poor countries have the capacity to make good products more cheaply than rich countries, they find the gates of these same rich countries locked against them." "but when countries do open their markets – often as conditions within World Bank and IMF loans – they are sometimes flooded with exports from rich countries."

The principals upon which these world organizations are based must be reversed. Treating all nations the same only works well between countries which have a similar level of economic development. Treating domestic and foreign companies the same works to the advantage of the developed nations and their multi-national corporations and prevents third world governments from stimulating their own economies by buying local.

Governments must be allowed to regulate within their own borders. National and local decision making must be permitted. Developing countries should be allowed to prevent foreign government subsidized agricultural products from entering their borders.

Considering the fact that major corporations worked with the U.S. government to create the World Trade Organization in its present form, and considering the way that they operate throughout the world, I believe that it is relevant next to discuss the issue of corporate crime.

Corporate crime is a very serious problem of global proportions.

The law department of Duke University published an article dated 1/13/17 titled: "The endless cycle of Corporate Crime and Why It's So Hard to Stop". The article recounts the following:

- Wells Fargo Bank being fined 185 million dollars for opening nearly two million bank and credit card accounts on behalf of their customers, with all the associated bank fees – without their customers' consent.
- An estimated 200 million dollars in fines for conduct associated with the 2008 financial collapse.
- Insider trading among what is described as "hedge fund kings".
- General Motors covering up faulty ignition switches.
- Volkswagen for setting up a system in its vehicles which cheats on emissions tests.
- British Petroleum's negligence in the Deep Water Horizon oil spill in the Gulf of Mexico.
- Insider trading waves back in the 1980's.
- Insider trading today.
- Lehman Brothers using accounting tricks to hide its debt.
- Enron using accounting tricks to hide its debt.

They even note a book on Corporate Crime: "Capitol Offenses: Business Crime & Punishment in America's Corporate Age" by Buell

The article refers to cases against many of the major banks, and giants in other industries; auto, pharmaceutical, energy, technology and aviation industries, and refers to a Manhattan Institute report that found that between 2004 and 2014, there were 303 non prosecution agreements (large fines), and that as of 2015, 16 of the Fortune 100 companies were undergoing this type of prosecution.

The article notes several recent attempts to control this problem and they ask the question: "Why does business crime continue to flourish despite ever-expanding efforts to fight it?" and they go on to discuss their thoughts on this matter, questioning "how society applies criminal law to business", noting that "There are still many unseemly behaviors that are tolerated in business."

I believe it was the excellent author Thom Hartman who recounted in his book "Unequal Protection" the early history of the British Empire, explaining that in the early days, England could in no way afford to have a standing army until companies established profitable foreign trade and were then taxed by their government, and it was only because of the tax revenues collected from British companies that England then eventually acquired the ability to equip a military force which was able to conquer foreign lands and then re-organize those foreign economies to enrich England.

I believe that the U.S. did follow a similar logic of believing that corporations, by their success in foreign lands, would help to endow the national economy. Ironically, today we talk about transfer pricing methods used by Multi-National Corporations to link revenues to parts of the world where taxes are very low, and to link expenses to the U.S. where we have income taxes, thus avoiding to a very large extent, taxation by U.S. authorities.

So what we are left with is a corporate block that lobbies government officials, then bribes them with campaign contributions which are now unlimited due to the Supreme Court ruling on the "Citizen's United" case, (which needs to be overturned) and they direct public attention away from social problems (through corporate owned mass media) that are generated by corporate activity. See my book: "Unravelling the Puzzle of the Los Angeles Times".

The Corporations are now swimming in cash that they can't even spend (Stiglitz) and the U.S. government can't even seem to find enough money for infrastructure and higher education.

The Corporate block is controlled by directors, many of whom are members of the Council on Foreign Relations and are thus directly connected to the U.S. foreign policy establishment.

Around the world today, sweatshops are now common, with employees working untenable hours for extremely low wages, so that, for example, Americans and Europeans can wear low priced clothing. The book "Wall Street's Think Tank" recounts a story reported by the New York Times, that Walmart was directly responsible for "blocking a 2011 effort to improve fire safety in Bangladesh, noting that its representatives stated it was not "financially feasible" to do so. There are too many more examples of this type of behavior.

Robert Hinkley, a former corporate law partner in two of America's largest law firms argues that many social ills are created by corporations because of the way that the

160

corporate charter has been written. He notes that in Maine, where he lives, Section 716 of the business corporation act states:

"the Directors and Officers of a corporation shall exercise their powers and discharge their duties with a view to the interests of the corporation and of the shareholders"

Hinkley notes that this provision is the motive behind all corporate actions everywhere around the world, and when and if officers fail to follow this prescription, they can be sued by their shareholders.

There is no mention currently in corporate charters on the subject of Public Interest. For example, the issue of human rights, as well as any social or ethical issues are not included and therefore are irrelevant to the corporate charter.

Hinkley believes that this set of standards helps to explain why the war against corporate abuse is currently being lost, and he proposes changing corporate law to make directors personally responsible for any harms to the public interest. Hinkley writes that "we must challenge the myth that making profits and protecting the public interest are mutually exclusive goals". Robert C Hinkley is the author of the book "Time to Change Corporations: Closing the Citizenship Gap".

Hinkley proposes amending the Section 716 statement about corporations exercising their powers with a view to the interests of the corporation and their shareholders, by adding the following words: "but not at the expense of the environment, human rights, the public safety, the communities in which the corporation operates, or the dignity of its employees." Negligent failure to abide by these rules would result in the corporation, its directors and its officers being financially liable for all damages that they caused.

Note that a Harris Poll published in Newsweek in 2000, asked Americans which of the following two statements they supported more strongly:

1. Corporations should have only one purpose – to make the most profit for their shareholders – and pursuit of that goal will be best for America in the long run.

2. Corporations should have more than one purpose. They also owe something to their workers and the communities in which they operate, and they should sometimes sacrifice profit for the sake of making things better for their workers and communities.

Note that 95% of Americans who responded to this poll chose the second proposition.

It is quite a testimony to the power of corporations through corporate owned mass media and through lobbing in Washington, that 20 years after this poll was taken, we still find ourselves in this exact same predicament.

Also, corporations should be regulated on an international level. A global regulatory agency should be created within the United Nations, to monitor and to develop international standards. Such a body should have the authority to perform investigations and to assist local organizations with bringing cases against certain types of anti-social behavior. Such a body should also include a court that will have binding authority. Its purview should also include the sanctioning of monopoly and cartel behavior.

Foreign investment needs to be regulatable by host governments. The need to attract foreign investments must be balanced by the need to promote economic development and to move towards the eradication of poverty.

Countries must be able to ensure their own food security by being allowed to support their own agricultural sectors.

A foreign policy that is based on robbing from the poor to stuff the rich is a foreign policy that needs to change. People, wherever they live, have a right to live in dignity and peace, where justice reigns supreme.

Chapter 8 – Making the World Safe for Democracy – or, Understanding the Enemy

Iraq, Yugoslavia, Libya, Venezuela, Nicaragua, and Cuba have or had very generous welfare states which allowed for only a limited penetration by Multi-National Corporations, and they served as examples to the world that another approach is possible. Their very existence served as a threat to complete corporate world domination, and opened the door for the possibility that the world might revert back to the policies that produced more than double the current rate of economic growth, which at the same time, relegates would be billionaires to mere multi-millionaires. War was to be the answer to solve this dilemma.

It can be said that North Korea is run by crazy people, because they don't trust us, although others think that maybe they are still sore about the fact that in the Korean War, the U.S. had managed to kill 30% of the entire population of North Korea.

People can look at Iran and have the understanding that they are irrational because they are so anti-American, although others point to the time when they had a Parliamentary Democracy that was then overthrown by the United States because Iran had nationalized their oil, seeking to use the proceeds for the benefit of all of the Iranian people instead of to further enrich the rich directors of foreign oil companies. The exact same thing can be said, of course, about Venezuela and Libya.

Under the Sandinistas of Nicaragua, a non-communist government, they were teaching their people how to read, and they created food banks to ensure that their people would not go hungry in bad times – at least these were the findings of the United Nations. But by removing the desperation of these people, they become believers in the possibility of creating their own destiny instead of being de-facto slaves who ultimately are serving U.S. corporate commercial interests. Reagan's fight against the Sandinistas of Nicaragua was a fight against the principals of American President Franklin D. Roosevelt, as would be applied to a Central American country.

Quoted from the book Nemesis by Professor Chalmers Johnson: "it should be noted that since 1947, while we have used our military power for political and military gain in a long list of countries, **in no instance has Democratic government come about as a direct result.**"

ON U.S. WAR CRIMES – How did they manage to kill so many people?

Method #1 – intentionally cause disease:

During the 1991 war against Iraq, the U.S. bombed and thus destroyed 18 out of 20 Iraqi electricity generating plants and their water pumping and sanitation systems. Dr. Thomas Nagy, a professor at George Washington University studied declassified documents including one titled: "Iraq Water Treatment Vulnerabilities" dated 1/22/91. This document noted that Iraq's rivers "contain biological materials, pollutants, and are laden with bacteria. Unless the water is purified with chlorine, epidemics of such diseases as Cholera, Hepatitis and Typhoid could occur." Later documents show that sanctions against Iraq embargoed the importation of chlorine, which prevented the purification of drinking water.

In a 1995 edition of Airpower Journal, Colonel John A Warden III wrote about the destruction of the electric power facilities in Iraq, noting that this resulted in the shutting down of water purification and sewage treatment plants, and that as a result, epidemics of Cholera and Typhoid broke out leading to perhaps as many as 100,000 civilian deaths.

The Harvard School of Public Health suggested in May of 1991 that "at least 170,000 children under five years of age will die in the coming year from the delayed effects" of the destruction of the electricity plants.

Curiously, due to U.S. sanctions, Iraq was explicitly not permitted to import any of the parts needed to repair and rebuild its electrical and water purification systems.

In 1995 the United Nations Food and Agriculture organization wrote to the Lancet, a highly respected British medical journal, that 567,000 Iraqi children, by their estimates, in fact, had died as a result of the U.S. sanctions. Other estimates calculated that about that same number of adults had also died for this same reason.

The Geneva convention of 1949 states: "It is prohibited to attack, destroy, remove, or render useless objects indispensable to the survival of the civilian population." "Drinking water installations" were also specifically mentioned. This helps to explain why the U.S. government will not join the International Court of Justice. In 1998 in Rome, an international Criminal Court was established. 120 countries, including Russia, joined and 7 did not: Algeria, Libya, Qatar, Yemen, China, Israel and the United States voted against it. So the happy news is that because the U.S. did not agree to the join the international criminal court, their war criminals were outside of its jurisdiction and therefore fee as birds.

On 5/11/96 on the program 60 minutes, interviewer Lesley Stahl said to then Secretary of State Madeline Albright: "We have heard that a half million children have died as a result of the sanctions. That's more than died in Hiroshima." "Is the price worth it?" Secretary Albright responded: "I think this is a very hard choice, but we think the price is worth it."

Two different people who had been appointed to administer the Oil for Food program at two different times for the United Nations, resigned in protest. Denis Halliday resigned in September of 1998 and Hans von Sponeck quit in protest in February of 2000. Both quit because under this supposed humanitarian program, masses of people would needlessly die of illness and starvation.

One of the problems with this program was that 34% of the proceeds were sent to Kuwait for repayment of war damage claims, and 13% of the proceeds were sent to Kurdish authorities in Northern Iraq, while Iraqi children died from lack of potable water. The United States government oversaw what was being ordered for import into Iraq and they were able to prevent the import of anything they wanted to prevent. Professor Joy Gordon of Fairfield University studied the sanctions and noted that in the winter of 2001 the following items were included in what was denied entry: dialysis, dental and firefighting equipment, water tankers which could distribute water to the population, and milk and yogurt making equipment.

Hans von Sponeck noted that the "oil for food" program was inadequate on three counts; the program allowed for only $252.00 per person, making it financially inadequate, less than 4% of that was earmarked for public education, and there was an inordinate delay in the arrival of items. An earlier director of this program,

Benon Sevan also criticized the United States for holding up needed equipment for Iraq.

An important article appeared in the Canadian website Global Research titled: "The United Nations and its Conduct During the Invasion and Occupation of Iraq". It was written by Denis Halliday the U.N. Humanitarian Coordinator in Iraq from 1997 to 1998. This article was written on 3/23/18. In 2018, Halliday writes that today we find almost total political and social chaos. Regarding the reconstruction and investment in infrastructure in Iraq, Halliday noted that little has been done, in spite of the fact that the U.S. was somehow able to manage to build 14 U.S. military bases inside Iraq.

Halliday offered the following assessments about the 2003 U.S. invasion of Iraq:

- The U.S. employed hundreds of tons of missiles and shells containing depleted Uranium, which resulted in epidemics of cancer. (particularly in southern Iraq)
- The 2003 invasion of Iraq was a complete violation of international law.
- War crimes were committed.
- "The breakdown of personal security, social services, health care, education, and basic needs has been almost total."

Halliday noted that under international law, an occupying force has the following obligations:

To uphold the domestic rule of law, to protect State and private property, and to protect the safety and the wellbeing of the civilian population. But he notes:

"They allowed, even facilitated, a complete breakdown in law and order. They stood back as looting and destruction in the cities and towns of Iraq took place. As days became weeks and months, they neglected to meet the basic needs of the people including food, housing, water, power, health care, education and employment."

Method #2 – intentionally cause mass starvation:

The U.S., with veto power under the small handful of nations that comprise the United Nations Security Council, designed a program to deliberately cause mass starvation in Iraq. A program was devised called the "Oil for Food Program" which ran from December of 1996 through November of 2003 – seven years out of the 13 years under which Iraq had been under sanctions.

Although this program was referred to as a humanitarian program, this program was funded entirely by Iraqi oil proceeds. The Iraqi oil producing infrastructure had been severely damaged during the first gulf war. Iraqi assets were frozen by the international banking industry, and there was no allocation to rebuild and repair the Iraqi oil industry in any significant way, so there was not sufficient oil revenue that could be produced by their oil industry.

This program, according to Hans von Sponek, who was in charge of it for a time, was able to provide on average, 33 cents per day per Iraqi citizen in order to provide enough food for human survival. It is of course no wonder that in the first half of the 1990's malnutrition and morbidity skyrocketed in Iraq.

In 2005 Hans von Sponek wrote a book about this program titled: "A Different Kind of War – the U.N. Sanctions Regime in Iraq". I quote: "Had there been a genuine concern for the welfare of the Iraqi people, the warnings by Secretaries-General Perez de Cuellar and Boutros Boutros-Ghali about the deteriorating circumstances in Iraq would have been taken more seriously."

Von Sponek noted that Dennis Haliday quit because in his view, the "Oil for Food" program was "A criminally flawed and genocidal U.N. Security Council Iraq policy". In this context, by U.N. Security Council, we mean the United States and England.

Iraq was prohibited from trading with its neighbors, or with any country in the world, and the citizens of Iraq were wholly dependent on the U.N. Security Council (the U.S.) for their survival. Von Sponek noted that from 1996 to 2003, with the exception of 2001, the value of goods that arrived in Iraq were far less than the amounts budgeted by the Iraqi government and the U.N. Von Sponek noted: "Such a situation should have) (led to an early increase in a permissible funding and the easing of the burocratic controls to speed up arrivals of essential supplies in Iraq. This did not happen."

"The U.S. and U.K. governments insisted that the blame for the inability to utilize allocated funds lay entirely with the government of Iraq. This is a serious misrepresentation of the facts, since there were no willful delays in the ordering of humanitarian supplies on the part of the Iraqi government."

Von Sponek noted that the major cause for under utilization of available resources was the complicated procurement process and the blocking of ordered supplies. "These are facts which cannot be dismissed by using references to the dictatorial regime of Saddam Hussein."

No resources were allocated for education and professional training, nor for the improvement of government institutions.

So the plan was to cause a die out of Iraqi citizens, not only by disease, which was indicated earlier, but also by mass starvation, and this is a plan that worked. So when the U.S. puts sanctions on other countries, there is never any short supply of cruelty.

Who was running the show? Because he was the person in charge of the Oil for Food program, there were two observation groups in Iraq who were observing the living conditions around the country, who were to report to Von Sponek's group. Von Sponek discovered that one of these groups was instead reporting to U.N. headquarters in New York instead of to the Humanitarian Coordinator in Bagdad.

"Managerially this made no sense and spelled disaster. It constituted an untenable obstacle to carrying out daily monitoring responsibilities in an efficient manner." He wrote that requests for changes in the reporting fell on deaf ears. His direct supervisor "cited a demand from the UN Security Council (U.S. & England (my emphasis added) that it wished to have the Multidisciplinary Observation Unit report to the UN Secretariat.) (Much later, in the winter of 1999, during a visit to the UN Headquarters, I brought this serious structural anomaly to the attention of Secretary-General Kofi Annan. He looked at me in astonishment. "This is difficult to believe" he said." "The Secretary-General was quick to reassure me that he shared my concern and would do something about what can only be described as a managerial nightmare. This reality, unfortunately, did not change during my tenure in Bagdad."

There has been much written about a method #3 – causation of conflict among different groups within Iraq to create a civil war. I believe that happened but I haven't found iron clad proof enough to write about it.

But with a now impoverished and uneducated population, Iraq's oil wealth can be stolen with greater ease.

Author and Professor Noam Chomsky noted that what the U.S. did to Iraq was far worse even than the Mongol invasions of Genghis Kahn in the early thirteenth century.

On January 3rd, 2020, the U.S. military killed Iranian general Suleimani in an airport in Iraq with a drone fired missile. In the discussion about this event, the Prime Minister of Iraq, Adil Abdul-Mahdi said: "Trump asked me to mediate with Iran – and then he kills my invitee." When reporters asked U.S. Secretary of State Mike Pompeo – wasn't Suleimani invited to Iraq by an intermediary of the Iraqi Prime Minister?, Pompeo responded with: "Would you believe such nonsense?" Not long before this, Mike Pompeo told RT: "(When) I was CIA Director, we lied, we cheated, we stole. We had entire training courses.

The Iranian minister of foreign affairs Mohammad Javad Zarif was going to come to the U.N. headquarters in New York to address the Security Council about this matter, but he was refused an entry visa to the U.S., in spite of the U.N. charter which provides that foreign representatives must be provided access to the U.N. headquarters in New York City and also in Geneva.

The Iraqi parliament, by majority decision then ruled that all foreign troops must leave Iraq. So on 1/6/20 an apparently unsigned letter from Brigadier General William Seely III, the Marine Corps officer in command of the U.S. coalition against ISIS, addressed Mr. Abdul Amir, Deputy Director, Joint Operation Bagdad, Iraqi Ministry of Defense, stating that the U.S. is ready to withdraw its troops. The White House immediately called this a confusion, a mistake, and confirmed that the U.S. has no intention of withdrawing troops. President Trump even threatened extremely serious sanctions if the troops were to be made to leave.

So as of January, 2020, thirty years after the start of the first war in Iraq, Iraq, a country that is supposed to be a U.S. ally instead, is a country that is occupied by a foreign power – the United States, and U.S. oil companies, which would have not been given contracts under Saddam Hussein, are operating there now, making impressive profits on Iraq's natural wealth.

This is a form of modern colonialism. On colonialism, Professor Chalmers Johnson pointed out in his book "Nemesis", that with very few exceptions, the countries that were victims of nineteenth century imperialism remain poor to this day.

Colonialism has often been "justified" by racism.

The following is a quote from Professor Walter Rodney from his book "How Europe Underdeveloped Africa".

"All of the countries named as "underdeveloped" in the world are exploited by others; and the underdevelopment with which the world is now preoccupied is a product of capitalist, imperialist, and colonial exploitation. African and Asian societies were developing independently until they were taken over directly or indirectly by capitalist powers. When that happened, exploitation increased and the export of surplus ensued, depriving the societies of the benefit of their natural resources and labor."

Tragically, Professor Walter Rodney died when a bomb which had been planted in his car, which was meant to kill him, exploded.

Look at what happened to India;

On page 292 of the book "Late Victorian Holocausts" by Mike Davis :

"When the sans culottes stormed the Bastile (in 1789) the largest manufacturing districts in the world were still the

Yangzi Delta (in China) and Bengal (in India), with Lingan (modern Guang Dong and Guangzi) and coastal Madras not far behind." India alone produced one quarter of world manufactures. On page 22 of "Empire" by Ferguson, he notes that India was a "vast and economically advanced subcontinent" which produced close to a quarter of the total planetary output of manufactured goods, compared with Britain's 3%.

On the effects of British Imperialism on India, Chalmers Johnson points out that:

"Given that for two centuries – between 1757 and 1947 – there was no increase at all in India's per capita income, that in the second half of Victoria's reign, between thirty and fifty million Indians perished in famines and plagues brought on by British mis-rule, and that from 1872 to 1921 the life expectancy of ordinary Indians fell by a staggering 20 percent, the idea that India benefited from British imperialism is at least open to question."

Philip McMichael, Professor of Development Sociology at Cornell University also quotes from the work of Mike Davis, and he discusses a food security issue which occurred during the last quarter of the nineteenth century in India and explains how the same dynamics are creating the very same results today, yet on a wider scale.

In the last quarter of the nineteenth century a devastating drought hit tropical regions around the world. India originally had a village grain reserve system to deal with bad crop years, but it was dismantled by England under their colonial rule. I will quote from Professor McMichael's article titled: "The World Food Crisis in Historical Perspective." From Global Research:

Prior to the British Raj, "Before the creation of a railroad-girded national market in grain, village-level food

174

reserves were larger, patrimonial welfare more widespread, and grain prices in surplus areas better insulated against speculation." Davis notes that transport systems, including the telegraph and its coordination of price hikes, regardless of local conditions, enabled merchants along the line to transfer grain inventories from the drought-stricken hinterland to hoarding centers.

Through this device, India was "force marched into the world market", and between 1875 and 1900, the worst years of Indian famine, grain exports rose from three to ten million tons annually, an amount equivalent to the annual nutrition of twenty—five million people, coinciding with the rough estimate of twelve to twenty-nine million deaths during this period. As Davis remarks, "Londoners were in effect eating India's bread" and quotes an observer, who wrote: "It seems an anomaly, that, with her famines on hand, India is able to supply food for other parts of the world." Davis noted the "perverse consequence of a unitary market was to export famine, via price inflation, to the rural poor in grain-surplus districts."

To quote Professor McMichael again: "The colonial era set in motion an extractive relation between Europe and the rest of the world, whereby the fruits of Empire displaced non-European provisioning systems, as the colonies were converted into supply zones of food and raw materials to fuel European capitalism. Professor McMichael is author of a number of books, including "Development and Social Change", "Contesting Development", and "Food Regimes and Agrarian Questions".

The U.S. today is engaging in the very same or similar types of activities that were rampant in prior centuries by the European colonial powers - England, Spain, France, Portugal, Holland and Belgium.

A college professor I once had, Bhuwan Joshi had a very different analysis of the Nazis. His thought was that they were the logical progression of European colonialism, where a European power tries to colonize the other colonizers. Joshi thought that the use of the term colonialist was odd considering that what was being called colonies were places where there were already people living there – so that couldn't exactly be a colony. It had to be something else.

American colonialism takes a different form than earlier forms. It is economic colonialism, but it attains the same results. By conservative estimates, approximately one billion people today are nutritionally insecure. "Democracy" is safe, indeed.

GEO POLITICAL ISSUES

For studies in Geo Politics, I would highly recommend authors F William Engdahl and Michel Chossudovsky.

The book "Towards a World War III Scenario" by Michel Chossudovsky provides quotes from a 2005 document from the U.S. Joint Chiefs of Staff:

"Integration of conventional and nuclear forces is therefore crucial to the success of any comprehensive strategy. This integration will ensure optimal targeting, minimal collateral damage, and reduce the probability of escalation." Also "To maximize deterrence of WMD use, it is essential US forces prepare to use nuclear weapons effectively and that US forces are determined to employ nuclear weapons if necessary to prevent or retaliate against WMD use.

Reference: Joint Chiefs of Staff "doctrine for joint nuclear operations" Joint Publication 3-12 http://zfacts.com/metapage/lib/zfacts_2005_03_15_jo int_nuclear_operations.pdf Washington D.C., March 2005

"Seeds of Destruction" by F William Engdahl is quite an important work. In its introduction, Kissenger is quoted as saying: "Control the oil and you control nations. Control the food and you control the people."

Controlling the food is an interesting issue. In 2007 and 2008 there was a huge increase in the price of food around the world. For example, in early 2008 the price of corn doubled, the price of wheat increased by 50%, and the price of rice increased by 70%.

An article in "The Economist" titled "The End of Cheap Food" noted that by the end of 2007, the food price index that they were using was at its highest point since price tracking started in 1845. Food prices had risen by 75% from 2005 to 2007. Much of this price increase was attributed to bio-fuel development in the United States.

With the rise in prices, Cargill's profits rose in 2007 by 36%, Archer Daniel Midland's profits rose by 67% and Bunge's profits rose by 49%. In the first quarter of 2008, Cargill's net profits rose by another 86% more, Archer Daniel Midland's profits were up another 55%, and this time Bunge's profits rose by 189%.

Fertilizer companies also participated. In 2007 Potash Corporation's profits increased by 72%, Mosaics's profits increased by 141%, and during the 1st quarter of 2008, Potash's net income rose by 186% and Mosaic's net income rose by more than 1,200%. Seed and Agro

Chemical companies also hit the big time. In 2007 Monsanto saw a 44% rise in profits, DuPont 19% and Syngenta 28%. The rise in these farm input materials explains why the rise in food prices did not result in rising profits for farmers.

Meanwhile, on the other side of the world, starting with when India first joined the WTO in 1995, up to 2007, reportedly 140,000 Indian farmers had committed suicide because they could not pay back their loans to the seed and pesticide companies. By 2012, the estimated number of farm suicides in India grew to a total of 200,000 people.

A 2014 article titled "Monsanto's GMO Creations Caused 291,000 Suicides in India." From Global Research, written by Mike Barrett, blames non viable crops grown from agribusiness patented seeds as the major cause of farm debt leading to mass suicide.

"Biotech sells seeds that either don't grow or lead to the development of unstoppable super weeds and super bugs. Subsequently, Biotech urges and nearly forces farmers to purchase Roundup and other herbicidal chemicals which the farmers can ill afford."

"We are ruined now, said one dead man's 38-year old wife. "We bought 100 grams of BT cotton. Our crop failed twice. My husband had become depressed. He went out to his field, lay down in the cotton and swallowed insecticide."

Despite serious warnings from research scientists, the U.S. Government decided that bio tech companies will regulate themselves. According to Engdahl, in his book "Seeds of Destruction" the most significant source of financing for the Biotech sector was the Rockefeller Foundation, and the Rockefeller family is closely linked with the Council on Foreign Relations, having been one of its main founders and having presided over it for many years.

In 2007 and 2008, rising food prices caused food riots in Italy, Uzbekistan, Morocco, Guinea, Mauritania, Senegal, West Bengal, Indonesia, Zimbabwe, Burkina Faso, Cameroon, Yemen, Jordan, Saudi Arabia, Egypt, Mexico, Argentina, and Haiti.(Philip McMichael 7/15/09).

McMichael reported in 2009 that about 70% of countries in the global South are now net food importers, and Engdahl believes that this is the result of a deliberate strategy by the American Foreign Policy Establishment.

From Engdahl's book "Seeds of Destruction", he notes in chapter 12 that in 1998 Delta & Pine Land Seed Company, with financial backing from the U.S. Department of Agriculture had won a joint patent with the U.S. Government for Gurt or Terminator Technology. This joint patent, U.S. patent number 5723765 titled "Control of Plant Gene Expression" allowed programming a plant's DNA to kill its own embryos – seeds. This patent applies to plants and seeds of all species.

For thousands of years, farmers have saved seeds generated by their crops so that they will be able to plant the next harvest. With these kinds of seeds, farmers instead will need to buy all their seeds every year from the seed company, making them totally dependent on the seed company whether they can afford it or not.

To quote from Engdahl's book:'

"in a June 1998 interview, USDA spokesman Willard Phelps had declared the U.S. government Policy on terminator seeds. He explained that the USDA wanted the technology to be "widely licensed and made expeditiously available to many seed companies." He added that the government's aim was "to increase the

179

value of proprietary seed owned by U.S. seed companies **and to open up new markets in second and third world countries**." (emphasis added) The USDA together with Delta & Pine Land then proceeded to apply for terminator patents in 78 countries.

Engdahl's book goes on to describe what he sees as a relationship between Kissenger's stated population control policies in the developing world, what had earlier been referred to as AS NSSM 200 in 1974, the Rockefeller Foundation's support for gene technologies in targeted developing countries, and the development of a gene technology which would allow multi-national corporations to own patents to seed varieties for vital food crops – the basis of life itself.

ON LIBYA AND AFRICA

In his book "The Globalization of War", Michel Chossudovsky discusses the NATO war on Libya with a different kind of analysis. He noted that the Al-Jamaa_Al-Islamiyyah, the Libya Islamic Fighting Group was an integral part of the Libyan "Opposition" that NATO was protecting and it was allied with Al Quaeda.

This type of analysis matches with a CNN report by Angela Dewan dated 9/14/16 titled: "Britain's Libya intervention let to growth of Isis, inquiry finds." That article reported that the Parliamentary Foreign Affairs Committee of the British house of Commons found that "the British government failed to identify that the threat to civilians was over stated and that the rebels included a significant Islamist threat."

Chussodovsky noted that by late August 2011, about one week before Tripoli was conquered by NATO, NATO had reported that from the start of the war in March, through to that point in August, that NATO had more than 7,700 strike sorties. "Multiply the number of strike sorties by the average number of missiles or bombs launched by each of the planes and you get a rough idea of the size and magnitude of this "humanitarian" military operation. A French Dassault Mirage 200 for instance, can transport eighteen missiles under its wings."

Libya was the most prosperous country in Africa, with the possible exception of the Republic of South Africa. Gaddafi had dropped the U.S. dollar and was attempting to develop a new pan African currency backed by gold. Libya had a very generous welfare state.

Under Gadaffi, in Libya:

- Education was free.
- Medical care was free
- Newlyweds received $50,000.00 from the government.
- Gasoline inside Libya was only 14 cents per liter.
- Gender equality was achieved.
- Libya ranked 53rd in the world in the U.N.'s Human Development Index.
- The Libyan government had no debt at all.
- The Food & Agriculture Organization (FAO) reported that undernourishment in Libya was experienced by less than 5% of the population.

All of this sounds good enough, but wealthy corporate directors were not getting any richer under these arrangements. Just a quick comparison with that last statistic – a September 2018 report from the United State's Department of Agriculture estimated that 11.8% of

American households are food insecure, and the U.S. government has a debt of more than 21 trillion dollars.

Based on information presented here, the stated position of NATO – that it was a humanitarian intervention – falls apart. Chussodovsky pointed to four goals that were achieved with the destruction of Libya;

#1. Libya has two to three times as much oil as does the United States, and the war was waged in order for NATO allies to take possession of Libya's oil reserves.

#2. 11% of Libya's oil exports went to China. China was involved in oil exploration activities in Libya through the China National Petroleum Corporation (CNPC). China had a workforce in Libya at the time of approximately 30,000 people. By supporting fundamentalist Islamic armed militias, the Chinese were forced to leave the country, which made it safe for the West to take it over at a later time.

#3. The idea was also to dismantle Libya's financial institutions so that billions of dollars of Libyan financial assets in foreign banks could then be confiscated.

#4. The idea was to establish U.S. hegemony in North Africa, which was historically dominated by the French, and to a lesser degree Spain. The belief is that Washington will attempt to weaken political links of Tunisia, Morocco and Algeria from France, and try to install pro-U.S. governments there.

The idea stated by Chussudovsky is that the U.S. is prepared in the short run to share influence with France with the long term goal being to exclude France, transforming Francophone Africa into a U.S. sphere of influence.

Africa is rich in oil, natural gas, gold, uranium, diamonds, and other important minerals. "U.S. puppet regimes have been installed in several African countries which historically were in the sphere of influence of France (and Belgium) including The Republic of Congo and Rwanda. Several countries in West Africa are slated to become U.S. proxy states."

Some of this analysis seems to be backed up by the very important book "Tomorrow's Battlefield – U.S. Proxy Wars and Secret Ops in Africa" by Nick Turse. To quote from that book: "the U.S. military, according to Tom Dispatch's analysis, is involved with more than 90% of Africa's fifty four nations."

This book was published in 2015 and I quote:

"What We Are Doing" the title to a December 2013 military document obtained by Tom Dispatch, offers answers to questions that Africom has long sought to avoid" "From 2008 to 2013, the number of missions, exercises, operations, and other activities under Africom's purview sky rocketed from 172 to 546," "Since 2011 U.S. Army Africa alone has taken part in close to one thousand "activities' across Africa.

Africom is The United States Africa Command, one of the eleven unified combatant commands of the United States Armed Forces. According to Wikipedia, Africom It is responsible for U.S. military operations, including fighting regional conflicts and maintaining military relations with 53 different African nations.

So this demonstrates that the U.S. has a lot of plans in Africa. Now we take a very brief look at the Middle East.

In 2007 Democracy Now interviewed Wesley Clark, a 4-star U.S. Army General, who was the Supreme Allied

Commander of NATO during the War in Yugoslavia. In that interview, General Wesley Clark stated the following:

"About ten days after 9/11, I went through the Pentagon and I saw Secretary Rumsfeld and Deputy Secretary Wolfowitz. I went downstairs just to say hello to some of the people on the Joint Staff who used to work for me, and one of the generals called me in. He said, "No. no." He says, "We've made the decision we're going to war with Iraq." This was on or about the 20th of September. I said, "We're going to war with Iraq? Why?" He said, "I don't know." He said, "I guess they don't know what else to do." So I said, "Well, did they find some information connecting Saddam to Al-Qaeda?" He said, No, no." He says, "There's nothing new that way. They just made the decision to go to war with Iraq."

"So I came back to see him a few weeks later, and by that time we were bombing in Afghanistan. I said "Are we still going to war with Iraq?" And he said, "Oh, it's worse than that." He reached over on his desk. He picked up a piece of paper. And he said, "I just got this down from upstairs" – meaning the Secretary of Defense's office – "today." And he said, "This is a memo that describes how we're going to take out seven countries in five years, starting with Iraq, and then Syria, Lebanon, Libya, Somalia, Sudan and finishing off, Iran." I said, "Is it classified?" He said, "Yes sir." "Well, don't show it to me."

What an amazing coincidence – this 2007 story from General Wesley Clark and what happened after that in this "troubled region".

Concerning the subject of Geo-Politics, what F. William Engdahl wrote on the back of his excellent book "Manifest Destiny" is most instructive;

"George Orwell's famous novel, 1984 is a masterful fictional account of a state which imposes cognitive dissonance on its citizens to control their perception of reality. It is summed up in the statement, "War is Peace; Freedom is slavery; Ignorance is strength." The story of this book, Manifest Destiny, is an account of how agencies of US intelligence including the CIA and State Department, in collaboration with private "democracy" NGO's developed and refined techniques of Orwellian doublethink or cognitive dissonance to create a series of regime changes around the world that sounded noble, democratic, but in reality were not.

William Engdahl describes the background beginning in the 1980's with Reagan's CIA Director leading to creation of a series of private NGO's to covertly manipulate aspirations for freedom and democracy from Poland and other communist countries in the late 1980's to the Soviet Union to Yugoslavia and China. The book details the refinement of what came to be called Color Revolutions by the early years of this century in Ukraine, Georgia and later with the US-orchestrated Arab Spring. It's an account of how elite circles in the USA and Europe along with their think tanks refined methods to impose a new tyranny on countries from Ukraine to Egypt to Libya and beyond. The aim was to use democratic aspirations of ordinary people, often youth, to topple regimes") ("This is an almost incredible chronicle of how select NGO's speak about freedom, human rights, democracy in order to bring war, violence and terror. This book is a must read for anyone wanting to truly understand world events of the past three decades or more."

Chapter 9 – What We Can Do

The following is a quote from "Democracy in America?" by professors Benjamin Page and Martin Gilens: "the megadonors of both parties tend to agree in opposing certain policies that most Americans favor. These include important policies related to government budgets, international trade, social welfare spending, economic regulation, and taxes"

The wealthy actually pay most of the taxes now. This is because the wealth and income are so unevenly distributed. A recent book by economist Thomas Piketty called Capital, was based on a study by the author, on France, over a 200 year period. His conclusion is that Capital accumulates wealth faster than the rate of growth of an economy. This means that without redistributive government policies, with unregulated capitalism (more or less what we have today), societies will, over time, devolve into what we see commonly in third world countries all around the world, where there are a few fabulously wealthy people living in a sea of human misery. This book "Capital" was lauded by many major economists. It did not go unnoticed.

So the very wealthy want small government because under the current developing scenario, they are paying for it, and they would rather keep that money for themselves. Also, the government has to power to tax them. The wealthy people who are right wing political operatives wish to benefit from all of the developments of human civilization but not have to pay a single penny for the price of civilization. It's ok to have a sea of humanity working and creating the wealth of a nation, but what do they get paid, by their company and also by their government?

Today the percentage of GDP dedicated to paying wages is the lowest that it has been since the great depression.

They cleverly call themselves job creators, but it's simply not true. Economists Michael Hudson and Joseph Stiglitz have observed that major corporations and wealthy individuals are sitting on hoards of cash. They don't want to expand businesses because there is not much demand. There is not much demand because although the economy has seen a lot of growth over the last 40 years, wages for the 99% have seen zero growth, and we also have many idle hands – the unemployed, who could add more to the national economy if only they had the chance.

How can we change this? We can go back to more progressive taxation which we had until Reagan. The economy grew at double the rate under progressive taxation than it does today. Progressive, meaning that each layer of income is taxed at a progressively higher rate.

We also need to vigorously enforce anti-trust policies which are highly correlated with economic growth. We need to re-regulate finance, which is also correlated with a higher rate of economic growth.

We need to break up the media corporations so that we can have a greater public market place of ideas. We essentially need to reverse the changes made beginning with Ronald Reagan in order to have the kind of economic growth we had before Ronald Reagan's administration. But nothing will be possible without campaign finance reform.

To quote once again from "Democracy in America?":

"Ordinary citizens simply do not have a significant voice in policy making. They are drowned out by the affluent and by organized interest groups – especially by business groups and corporations."

"On many important issues, affluent and wealthy Americans seriously disagree with average citizens. Most Americans want the wealthy to pay more taxes, but the wealthy do not. Most Americans want tighter regulation of big corporations and financial institutions, but the wealthy disagree. Wealthy Americans also tend to oppose government help with jobs, wages, health care, education, retirement pensions, and other matters of great concern to average Americans."

Note that A few years before the Trump administration lowered the tax rate on corporations and the rich, nearly two thirds of Americans in opinion polls had already expressed the belief that corporations and the wealthy are not paying their fair share of taxes.

The National Academy of Sciences performed a study on ethics and wealth. They concluded that higher social class predicts increased unethical behavior.

So the least ethical among us are literally running our society. In a country with better functioning democratic institutions, something like this, what we are currently seeing in the U.S., would not be able to happen.

Obviously, we need to get money out of politics. Since the 1970's campaign finance laws have been reversed by the Supreme Court. And guess what happened? To quote again from "Democracy in America?":

"In the 1980's about 10 percent of all campaign spending came from one-tenth of one percent (0.01) of the voting age population. By 2012, more than 40 percent of spending came from this tiny sliver of wealthy Americans." "In 2012, 93% of super-pac money came from only 3,318 people, and more than half of all super-pac money came from just 159 individuals."

I would highly recommend this book "Democracy in America?" as it is filled with the most salient information on the democracy deficit today, and it proposes many solutions. It comes very well documented by these two University professors Benjamin Page and Martin Gilens.

The knockout punch was the Citizens United ruling in 2010. Corporations can be treated as fictitious persons for the purpose of being able to enter into contracts. The Supreme Court then declared that corporations have the same constitutional rights as do humans, and that spending on politics amounts to "speech", so that corporate donations to political campaigns is "freedom of speech". Next came the "Speech Now" case, where the Supreme Court ruled that "Independent" expenditures to a political campaign cannot be in any way regulated. So now voila! Unregulated campaign contributions by corporations is now legal.

So this has to be overturned. The Supreme Court judges who ruled for this need to be impeached. Impeachment cannot happen under Republicans, so in order to try to save democracy, we have to start out by relying on the Democrats – who are also corrupted by this system.

As of 2016, 16 states and about 700 municipalities supported a constitutional amendment to overturn this Citizens United ruling. In September, 2014, a majority of the U.S. Senate voted in support of a constitutional amendment stating that corporations are not people (of course they are not) but it did not make it all the way through the process, into law.

We need campaign finance reform, as studies in Political Science show a direct correlation between the amount of money a campaign has to spend with the likelihood of that candidate winning the election.

Law professor Lawrence Lessig, the former director of the Edmond J Safra Center for Ethics at Harvard University came out with an excellent book on campaign finance reform titled "Republic Lost". I highly recommend that book. He came up with an idea where the government gives each citizen a voucher or stored value card worth $50.00 that each citizen can use towards any candidate or candidates. Page & Gilens add to this their idea that each candidate can receive these funds only if they would agree that this will be the only type of funding that they will accept. This would all be voluntary. There are approximately 235 million people today in the U.S. of voting age. If 200 million people each used a $50.00 voucher, that would total 10 billion dollars. Currently, presidential elections are financed with 3 billion – One Billion by Democrats, One Billion by Republicans, and One Billion by the extreme right-wing Koch Brothers and their very small group. So 10 Billion dollars of funding by the population would really be able to move the country towards one person one vote instead of one dollar one vote. This 50 dollars could also suffice for not only a presidential election but also a congressional election or two, as well.

Also, 10 billion dollars is not very much money to the federal government, especially in relation to the extreme and crucial importance of this matter. That 10 billion dollars would be for an election which happens every four years, so it would really add up to 2.5 billion per year for REAL democracy promotion.

As for 2.5 billion per year, I would like to draw your attention to an article in the New York Times dated 8/5/16 titled: "Do Oil Companies Really Need 4 Billion Per Year of Tax Payer's Money?". Our government is subsidizing the oil industry, which doesn't need to be subsidized. Some of that money would go a long way towards developing alternative energy systems that would save humanity from impending doom caused by global warming.

Full disclosure laws will need to be implemented for the traditional corrupt types of campaign financing methods.

The government will also need to fund alternative media outlets, since the major media corporations do not cover elections per say. Certainly not in respect to the question of why a candidate is a candidate – what are their ideas. No, they just cover who is ahead in the polls and just keep switching back and forth ad-infinitum between different campaigns. Of course, that does not provide any meaningful information to the people in order to establish rationally considered voting preferences.

Seeing that elections are important, perhaps there should also be some legislation requiring media companies to cover them. Professor Robert McChesney had noted in one of his many stellar books – that by not including any content in their coverage, the media companies impel candidates to spend more advertising dollars so that people will know something, anything, about them. Perhaps this process can best be described by the title of one of McChesney's books "Rich Media, Poor Democracy".

Many people today don't even know what they are voting for, which suits some people just fine, but the same cannot be said for the majority of the population.

Because it is the very wealthy who subvert the powers of government to prey on people in order to gain yet more wealth, - the wealth of others – those in a weaker position, the U.S. Government should put an absolute limit on how much wealth that individuals should be allowed to keep. The rest needs to accrue back to the government as wealth tax. This will kill the incentive to kill.

Now let's look at empathy and compassion. An article dated 5/23/2013 from Psychology Today notes that "Compassion Can Be Trained"

"Researchers have confirmed that both compassion and altruism can be cultivated with training and practice." "A new study by researchers at the Center for Investigating Healthy Minds at the Waisman Center of the University of Wisconsin-Madison shows that adults can be trained to be more compassionate." "Our fundamental question was, can compassion be trained and learned in adults? "Our evidence points to yes."

Michele Borba wrote a new book: Unselfie: Why Empathic Kids Succeed in Our All-About-Me World" The book offers tools for parents to teach their children to have more empathy and compassion for others.

Earlier we also looked at the idea of changing the Corporate Charter.

Change begins with a proper education of the public. As mentioned earlier, a 30 year long series of surveys by authors Benjamin Page and Marshall Bouton found that the general public are most interested in domestic affairs, and want the U.S. to be fair and just in its foreign affairs, giving the United Nations a central role as the overseer of international law. More democratization in America will result in a wiser foreign policy.

We are not as democratized as we should be, due to the nature of the mass media's performance. I will quote "Breaking the Sound Barrier" by Amy Goodman:

"Fairness and Accuracy In Reporting, a media watchdog group, did a study analyzing the majority of nightly news casts for the two weeks surrounding then – Secretary of State Colin Powell's speech for war before the United Nations on February 5, 2003. On the major evening newscasts on ABC, CBS, NBC and PBS, Fair found 393 interviews on the issue of war, of which only three were anti-war leaders. This is when a majority in the United States either opposed war or supported more time for inspections."

Goodman then argues: "This is not a mainstream media but an extreme media, beating the drums for war."

In an 8/1/2005 article by FAIR, a media watch organization, they reported that often times media magnates and board of director members have close links with military contractors. Not only that, but:

"NBC's owner General Electric designed, manufactured or supplied parts or maintenance for nearly every major weapon system used by the U.S. during the Gulf war – including the Patriot and Tomahawk Cruise Missiles, the Stealth Bomber, the B-52 Bomber, the AWACS plane and the NAVSTAR Spy Satellite System."

A 12/1/2008 article from the Columbia Journalism Review titled: "Above the Fold: Complex Analysis" discusses a 11/30/2008 article in the New York Times by David Barstow. Barstow's article revealed that the Pentagon recruited 75 retired military officers to appear as objective experts on ABC, CBS, NBC, CNN and Fox. These individuals were not only retired military officers. They were also either lobbyists, board members, senior executives or consultants to over 150 military contractors. The author of this article for the Columbia Journalism Review noted: "The networks reacted to that Times story with a stunning wall of silence."

Today only 6 corporations are responsible for at least 90% of our nation's mass media. The business model of mass media is to gain their earnings through advertising the products and services of major corporations. Because corporations control an estimated 50% of the wealth of this planet, this business plan results in major conflicts of interest whenever news is to be reported.

The book Giants by Professor Peter Phillips draws out the fact that major corporations today act as an integrated block. He writes about the great extent to which they invest heavily in each other and depend on each other for their investment earnings, and share the same board members in very many cases. So there are very serious issues when relying on the major news networks and newspapers, and ultimately it is Democracy itself which suffers, as the general public is exposed to "news" which turns out to be highly partisan.

This book "Giants" also looks at several organizations which have been created over the years, such as the Council on Foreign Relations for example, whose decision making membership is made up of people of the trans-corporate class, who plan together on ways to safeguard and increase their wealth by influencing tax policy, foreign policy, and other policies to their personal benefit.

U.S. foreign policy today, and since the end of world war II, is nothing better than a criminal enterprise of astronomical proportions.

How can the U.S. truly guard their national security?

- By being allies with all nations and all people of the world.
- By following the U.N.
- By re-defining National Interests to include the well-being of all people of the earth, and to also include human survival.
- By abstaining from doing in foreign countries anything that would be considered a crime against humanity, even if such things would make rich people richer.

- By doing what any ten year old child would do regarding the question of following the dictates of science regarding nuclear proliferation, global warming, and chemical pollution.

Example: A number of years ago, Ralph Nader discussed a line of bombers being promoted by Congress that the Pentagon did not even want, and he mentioned that the annual amount of money that was earmarked for that program would have been more than enough to prevent malnutrition around the world.

Nader's point was that by choosing to provide food for the hungry around the world, the U.S. would lose enemies and make new allies in the process, which would save the nation an enormous amount of money on national defense. That would be a thoughtful foreign policy objective.

We have layers upon layers of propaganda in our mass media. Here is a quote from Michel Chussodovsy from "America's War on Terrorism":

"war criminals continue to legitimately occupy positions of authority, which enable them to redefine the contours of the judicial system and the process of law enforcement. The process has provided them with a mandate to decide "who are the criminals", when in fact they are the criminals."

The process of further democratization of public policy can be achieved when increasing numbers of people discover the many highly professional alternative media sources, become better informed, and thus becoming a political force for change.

One of these sources is made up of a group of 25 colleges and universities under a program centered in the Sociology Department at Sonoma State University called Project Censored. They have put out a book every year for the last 40 years called Censored 2019, Censored 2018, etc., and they report each year on the top 25 stories that they say did not receive adequate news coverage in the main stream media.

Their stories are quite eye opening and are recommended reading for those who wish to be well informed. These stories are vetted 4 times by a well-resourced professional staff.

We are currently living in a golden era of information – and also of disinformation.

Post Script

You the reader have now read this account of unimaginable brutality and evil, perpetrated by your own government against innocent people around the world.

The people who are presiding over this tyranny are:

High level corporate executives who lobby our government and often time write the trade rules that other countries will have to follow.

The Republican Party.

The military and the "Intelligence" organizations who prosecute these actions – these crimes against humanity.

What do these groups all have in common? They are conservatives. What did we learn about conservatives?

They have a compassion and an empathy deficit.

But there is also one more group that is also responsible - the Democratic Party, who for whatever reason is in on this feeding frenzy.

People around the world are calling out in unimaginable agony and pain.

From shanty towns that arose because our government wanted to promote U.S. agribusiness overseas.

From prisons where people have become political prisoners because they wanted something better for their countrymen.

From failing cotton farms in India where the people were cheated by U.S. Agribusiness, U.S. farm subsidies, and the World Trade Organization.

From the victims of hunger and oppression around the world, who have to live under governments that work for the benefit of United States policies against the welfare of their own countrymen.

You who are reading this – humanity needs you. Become a voice for the voiceless. Spread the word, and let other people know about what is this tragedy which has a name - U.S. Foreign Policy.

Furthermore, this same voracious process is also happening to American citizens. We see it in a hollowed out economy with jobs shipped overseas. We see it in a government that puts all its money into the military with little left for public services. We see it in a corporate media that tells people to look the other way so they don't see what is occurring all around us.

SUGGESTED SOURCES FOR NEWS on the internet:

Accuracy in Media – AIM: Https://www.Aim.org

Alternet

Center for Media & Democracy

Center for Responsive Politics

Common Dreams

Consortium News

Democracy Now   www.DemocracyNow.Org
(They are also on Dish Network and Direct TV)

Fairness & Accuracy in Reporting (FAIR)

The Gray Zone

The Intercept

Jimmy Dore Show

Media Alliance: Https://media-Alliance.org

Media Matters: Www.MediaMatters.org/

Mint Press News

Naked Capitalism

National Security Archive George Washington University

Politico

Popular Resistance.Org

Progressive.Org

Project Censored

Pro Publica

Public Citizen

Ralph Nader Radio Hour: RalphNaderRadioHour.Com

RT (sponsored by the Russian government)

Redacted Tonight show on You-Tube (also RT)

Salon.Com

TruthDig.com

TruthOut.Org

Yes Magazine

You Tube program: Redacted Tonight also, Redacted VIP

United Nations News

A very good newspaper in the U.K, available on line: The Guardian

Suggested Readings:

Public Policy and Current Affairs:

The New Jim Crow by professor Michelle Alexander

by Professor Eric Alterman:

What Liberal Media?

The Conservatives Have no Clothes by Anrig

Books by Dean Baker, Economist

The end of Loser Liberalism

Social Security – the Phoney Crisis

Taking Economics Seriously

The Conservative Nanny State

False Profits

Rigged

Unequal Democracy by Bartels

Books by Phyllis Bennis:

Understanding the Palestine Israeli Conflict

Understanding the U.S. - Iran Crisis

Ending the U.S. War in Afghanistan

Calling the Shots

Books by William Blum

Killing Hope: U.S. Military & CIA Interventions since WWII

Rogue State

Freeing the World to Death

America's Deadliest Export

Michelle Borba - Unselfie - Why Empathic Kids Succeed

Labor's Untold Story by Boyer & Morais

Plan B 4.0 by Lester R. Brown

Full Planet, Empty Plates by Lester R Brown

The Public Bank Solution by Ellen Brown

Web of Debt by Ellen Brown

How Markets Fail by John Cassidy

Censored - 2018, 2017, 2016 and so on - Project Censored - Sonoma State University

Books by Economist, Professor Ha-Joon Chang:

Bad Samaritans

Kicking Away the Ladder

23 Things They Don't Tell You About Capitalism

Reclaiming Development – An Alternative Policy Manual

Books by Professor Noam Chomsky:

Hegemony or Survival

Failed States

Understanding Power

Deterring Democracy

Manufacturing Consent   by Professor Chomsky and Professor Herman

The Washington Connection and Third World Fascism

The Global Economic Crisis by Michael Chossudovsky

The Globalization of Poverty by Michael Chossudovsky

The Globalization of War by Michael Chossudovsky

America's War on Terrorism by Michael Chossudovsky

Towards a World War III Scenario by Michael Chossudovsky

Cable News Confidential   by Jeff Cohen

Diet for a Dead Planet by Christopher Cook

Books by Mark Curtis

Unpeople

Secret Affairs

Web of Deceit

Trade for Life

Take This Job & Ship It   Senator Dorgan

Reckless by Senator Dorgan

The Doomsday Machine by Daniel Ellsberg

Seeds of Destruction by F. William Engdahl

Manifest Destiny by F. William Engdahl

Myths Lies and Oil Wars by F. William Engdahl

Full Spectrum Dominance by F. William Engdahl

Gods of Money by F. William Engdahl

Target China by F. William Engdahl

Image & Realilty by Professor Norman Finkelstein

No Debate by Farah

The Record of the Paper – Professors. Falk & Friel

Israel - Palestine on Record by Professors Falk & Friel

Lies and the Lying Liars that Tell Them   by Senator Al
Franken

The Truth   by Senator Al Franken

America's Education Deficit and the War on Youth by
Henry Giroux

The War Comes Home: Washington's Battle Against
America's Veterans by Aaron Glantz

Books by Amy Goodman:

The Exception to the Rulers

Static

Standing up to the Madness

National Insecurity by Melvin Goodman

Empire's Workshop by Professor Greg Grandin

Great American Hipocrites by Glen Greenwald

With Liberty & Justice for Some by Glen Greenwald

Who Will Tell the People   by William Greider

Books by Thom Hartman

The Crash of 2016

Rebooting the American Dream

Unequal Protection

Screwed

Winner Take All Politics by Hacker & Pierson

Hope & Folly by Professor Preston, Professor Schiller and Professor Herman

Beyond Hipocracy   by Professor Herman

Hot by Mark Hertzgaard

Lords of Secrecy by Scott Horton

By economist Michael Hudson:

Super Imperialism – By Professor Michael Hudson

THE BUBLE & BEYOND by Professor Michael Hudson

Finance as Warfare

Killing the Host

J is for Junk Economics

Human Rights Watch – Annual World Report

The Warehouse Prison – John Irwin

Behind the Scenes at the WTO by Jawara & Fatoumata

Books by Professor Chalmers Johnson:

Blowback

Dismantling the Empire

The Sorrows of Empire

Nemesis

Free Lunch by David Kay Johnston

Perfectly Legal by David Kay Johnston

The Bush Agenda by Antonia Juhasz (Policy Analyst for 2 Senators)

The Tyrany of Oil by Antonia Juhasz

That Changes Everything by Naomi Klein

The Shock Doctrine by Naomi Klein

Field Notes from a Catastrophe by Elizabeth Kolbert

End This Depression Now by Professor Paul Krugman

The Conscience of a Liberal by Professor Paul Krugman

Everything for Sale by Robert Kuttner

Bank Occupation – Waging Financial War on Humanity – Stephen Lendman

Republic Lost – by Professor Lawrence Lessig

Six Degrees by Lynas

Economics Unmasked by Professors Max-Neef and Smith

The Death & Life of American Journalism by McChesney & Nichols

Blowing the Roof Off the 21st Century by McChesney

People Get Ready by McChesney & Nichols

I Rigoberta Menchu – an Indian woman in Guatemala By Rigoberta Menchu and Elizabeth Burgos-Debray

The Republican War on Science by Mooney

The Republican Brain by Mooney

Doing Democracy by Bill Moyer

Moyers on Democracy by Bill Moyers (a different person also named Bill Moyers)

Books by Ralph Nader

The 17 Solutions

No Contest

Cutting Corporate Welfare

Merchants of Doubt by Oreskes & Conway

What Government can do by Professors Page & Simmons

The Foreign Policy Disconnect by Page & Simmons

Democracy In America? By Page & Gillens

Armed Madhouse   by Greg Palast

The best Democracy Money Can Buy   by Greg Pallast

Tropic of Chaos by Parenti

Books by Professor Michael Parenti, PHD:

Democracy for the few

The force of Imperialism

Contrary Notions

History as Mystery

Profit Pathonlogy

The Sword and the Dollar

The End of Food by Thomas F Pawlick

   (There are two books with this same title by two

   Separate authors. This is the one that I read and can
recommend/.)

Stuffed and Starved   by Raj Patel

The Value of Nothing   by Raj Patel

Unholy Trinity by Richard Peet

Hope & Folly by Profs Preston, Schiller and Herman

Confessions of an Economic Hit Man by Perkins

Giants by Peter Phillips

Freedom Next Time by John Pilger

It takes a Pillage by Nomi Prins

Other Peoples' Money by Nomi Prins

Books by professor Robert Reich:

Aftershock

Saving Capitalism

Beyond Outrage

Super Capitalism

An Unbroken Agony by Robinson

A Theory of Global Capitalism by William I. Robinson

Global Capitalism & the Crisis of Humanity by William I Robinson

Hell and High Water by Joseph Romm

Books by Jeffrey Sachs, Economist:

The end of Poverty

Building the New American Economy

The Price of Civilization

Common Wealth

Culture, Inc.   by Professor Schiller

Wall Street's Think Tank by Laurence Shoup

Command and Control by Eric Schlosser

The Lost Soul of Higher Education by Professor Ellen Schrecker

Bio Piracy by Vandana Shiva

Treasure Islands by Shaxson

Social Dominance by Sidanius and Pratto

Unravelling the Puzzle of the Los Angeles Times by Danel Silver

Books by Economist - Professor Joseph Stiglitz;

The Price of Inequality

Re Writing the Rules of the American Economy

Globalization and its Discontents

The Three Trillion Dollar War

Freefall

Making Globalization work

Globalization and its Discontents Revisited

The Euro

In Search of Enemies by John Stockwell:

Lives Per Gallon by Terry Tamminen

Kill Anything that Moves by Nick Turse

The United Nations Today by the United Nations

The CIA as Organized Crime by Douglas Valentine

The Strength of the Wolf by Douglas Valentine

Yanis Varofakis, Economist:
The Global Minotar

And the Weak Suffer What They Must?

Adults in the Room

Whose Trade Organization? By Lori Wallach

University, Inc by Jennifer Washburn

Failed by Economist Mark Weisbrot

The Spirit Level by Wilkinson & Pickett

A Power Governments Cannot Suppress by Howard Zinn